Colonel Unthank's Norwich

A sideways look at the city.

CLIVE LLOYD

Colonel Unthank's Norwich
A sideways look at the city.

Clive Lloyd

Published in the United Kingdom by Clive Lloyd

colonelunthanksnorwich.com

First printed 2021

Designed by Karen Roseberry

I should start by explaining the title of this book to those of you who won't have seen my monthly blog posts. The site from which these articles are drawn (www.colonelunthanksnorwich.com) was named Colonel Unthank's Norwich because I once lived on the city's Unthank Road and became fascinated by the unusual name of the Unthank family, three of whom were colonels. They developed the land on which the Golden Triangle was built as described in a previous short book, Colonel Unthank and the Golden Triangle. On Twitter I also tweet about local history under the username of @ReggieUnthank, formed by adding the name of a favourite uncle. Reggie appears in one of these chapters.

In December 2015 I started my blog with a post on Norfolk's Stained Glass Angels. This was followed by several posts on the Wymondham-born designer of the Aesthetic Movement, Thomas Jeckyll, an article on Arts & Crafts houses in Norfolk, Art Nouveau buildings in Norfolk (not many of these), angels' pyjamas and a little more about the Arts & Crafts Movement. Angels apart, in these early outings I focussed on my long-standing fascination with the art and architecture of the late nineteenth/early twentieth century. Now flying under the banner of 'History, Decorative Arts, Buildings', I soon started to include more articles on Norwich buildings and this has become a major theme over the past five years.

Not being born in Norwich I have an incomer's curiosity for the way my adopted city came to look the way it does. Architect George Skipper's 'fireworks' are unmistakable but I soon learned to appreciate the quiet genius of Edward Boardman for introducing proto-modern commercial buildings into what was essentially a Late Medieval city. Before the railways brought foreign materials into a city based on chalk, Norwich was built with wood and thatch or, later, local brick and tile. Only those who could afford the transportation costs could afford stone, so prestige projects were based on the more ubiquitous substitute found in seams amongst the chalk – flint. Anyone long established here is likely to have forgotten the visitors' surprise (and hopefully delight) at seeing so many buildings constructed of intricately knapped flint. This city also arose from clay and several posts deal with the output of Gunton's Brickyard in Costessey, especially the fancy carved bricks that added decoration before detail was shunned in the age of steel and glass.

Other themes emerged from walking the city. From my arrival in the 1980s I wandered through Norwich. Drawn to the outskirts and Norwich-over-the-Water I just followed my nose and without knowing it became a psychogeographer, studiously avoiding the well-worn path. It was never my intention to write a head-on history of the city. I hope instead that this sense of drifting materializes in the book, explaining the eclectic selection of topics. Nevertheless, patterns emerge as the same names and places crop up in different contexts. In this way I learned more about the Dukes of Norfolk while researching the Duke Street Car Park than I did from rehearsing the timeline of the Howard family. The resulting book is a deliberately sideways look at Norwich.

Clive Lloyd
May 2021
colonelunthanksnorwich.com
Twitter: @ReggieUnthank

NORWICH DOORS

CONTENTS

THE BLOOD RED RIVER

NORWICH BRIDGES #1

Before the ring road redefined its shape, Norwich appeared on old maps as a leg-of-mutton (although some say it is shaped like a turnip). This shape was imposed upon the city by its twin defences comprised of the city walls that cupped the western side and the River Wensum that looped around the eastern flank. The river does not, however, join in neatly but cuts across part of the walled city, separating it into Norwich-over-the-Water and the commercial centre. The riverside is where many of the city's trades were concentrated so to walk along the meandering river is to retrace the fortunes of the city's industrial past; it also sets the scene for several of the articles to follow.

I began the first part of my journey at the head of navigation by turning into New Mills Yard off Westwick Street. This was the site of a mill, dated to 1410, that was replaced 300 years later by the New Mills that ground corn as well as raising water to the upper parts of the city. In the blog post I showed a photograph of George Plunkett's son Jonathan being measured against a flood marker, set into the wall, demonstrating how the river has inundated the city over the centuries. We will see the effects of flooding as we walk downstream. At New Mills, sluice gates regulate the water that flows upstream so the water is tidal only to this point. Upon the bridge is a fine late Victorian building erected by the council in 1897 to extract what energy it could from the meandering river. This is the Pump House or Compression House that had two water-powered and three electric-powered compressors, which pumped sewage down to Trowse; it also provided the energy to power machinery in the Norwich Technical Institute (now Norwich University of the Arts) a few hundred yards downstream.

The next crossing is St Miles' Bridge (named after the nearby parish church) also known as Coslany Bridge (named after the district), decorated with the City of Norwich coat of arms and dated 1804. Designed by James Frost, this was the city's first iron bridge, built 25 years after the world's first major iron bridge at Ironbridge, Shropshire. When I stood on St Miles bridge my feet were about the same level as the river during the 1912 flood that devastated the riverside industries and much of Norwich-over-the-Water.

In historical terms the bridge is important for connecting three of the industries that formerly sustained this city. First, on the north bank, the present-day public housing in Barnard's Yard is named for the Norfolk Iron Works of Barnard Bishop and Barnards whose several tall chimneys dominated the district of Coslany from the mid-nineteenth to the mid-twentieth century. One of Charles Barnard's early inventions was a machine for weaving wire netting, which is now conserved in the Museum of Norwich at The Bridewell. In 1846 Charles Barnard went into business with John Bishop to be joined 13 years later by his two sons, thus forming Barnard Bishop and Barnards, some of whose numerous domestic and agricultural items products were impressed with their symbol of four letters B and/or four bees. Other chapters in this book describe the ironwork designed by Wymondham-born Thomas Jeckyll but it was here that his drawings were made real.

On the opposite side of the bridge, unmissably spelled in Victorian Gothic lettering, is 'Bullard & Sons' Anchor Brewery'. Up to the mid-twentieth century it would have been even more conspicuous due to its tall industrial chimney decorated with the letters 'BULLARDS'. Now the former brewery is private housing. In 1912, Bullards was a victim of the 1912 floods that devastated this low-lying part of the city. At this period, it was possible to photograph the effects of the river's liability to overflow, providing a glimpse into the impact of flooding upon historically-important buildings along the riverside. Thankfully, Bullards beers

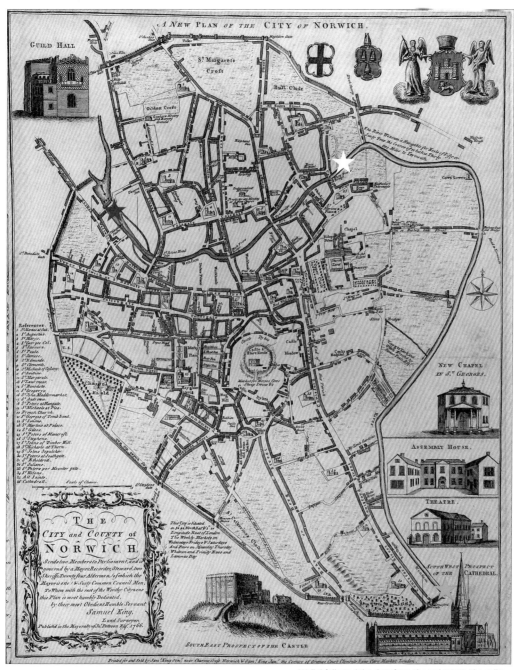

Walk 1 followed the river from the red star to the yellow;
Walk 2 continued down to the blue star.   King's map 1766

7

Compression House at New Mills

Coslany Bridge

didn't rely on water drawn from the dubious Wensum since they were able to take high quality water from their own artesian well.

The bright rose-madder colour in which the Anchor Quay buildings are now painted provides a vivid reminder of the third former trade. This was the dyeing industry that went hand in glove with the city's manufacture of textiles. If we were to drift away from the river, towards the city, we would quickly enter the Maddermarket district where dried madder roots were sold, but if we want to see where the dye was actually used we need to continue just a few hundred yards along the river bank.

Immediately before the next bridge, on the city side, are the former offices of the Norwich Electricity Company that replaced the old Duke's Palace Ironworks in 1892. At one time, the river would have provided water to cool the turbines but, after the Thorpe Power Station took over the generation of electricity in the 1920s, the Duke Street site was used for clerical and storage purposes. The curved, five-storey building has lain derelict for years although in 2006 a group of artists temporarily took it over during the Eastinternational exhibition. They covered the windows with red film and white lettering that spelled: 'norwich red/water of the wensum/tin mordant/madder'. Reflected in the water, this formulation for colouring fabric created the illusion

Anchor Quay in pink with curving Electricity Board buildings behind

that – once more – the dyeing industry 'made the river run red'. The original reason behind the red river comes a little downstream, for the story follows the course of the river.

This stretch of the Wensum on the city side is known as the Duke's Wharf and forms the river frontage of what was once the Duke of Norfolk's palace). According to Samuel King's 1766 map the palace once occupied most of a block between the modern day Anchor Quay and Blackfriars' Hall. It was here that Queen Elizabeth stayed when she came to Norwich in 1671 on one of her progresses. The house was the most sumptuous in East Anglia with room enough to accommodate the queen's retinue of 55. This did, however, require the duke to turn his indoor tennis court into a kitchen and

Red reflections in the Wensum ©Ann Christie

Proximity to the water meant that the cellars were always wet, which affected the foundations. The fate of the palace was sealed when the Mayor of Norwich, Thomas Havers, refused the duke permission to process into the city with his Company of Comedians so in 1711 the duke ordered the palace be pulled down. When the duke vacated his palace there was no road through his estate and no bridge across the Wensum as there is today. The present – but not the first – bridge to bisect the ducal waterfront was built when Duke Street was widened in 1972 as part of the plan to take traffic out of the city and on to the inner ring road. A rather utilitarian bridge, which leaves no headroom for a riverside walk, replaced the first and much more elegant cast-iron bridge of 1822. This bridge would have been lost to us were it not for the Norwich Society who bought and stored it until it could be re-used at the entrance to the Castle Mall car park on Market Avenue Now we have a marker for the exact location of the dyeworks, for in the early nineteenth century James

his large bowling alley (130 feet wide by 190 feet long) into several eating rooms. This conveys a sense of the scale of the splendid accommodation: however, not all was sweetness and light and it was the proximity of the palace to the river that caused problems. According to Thomas Baskerville in 1681, the palace was 'seated in a dung-hole place' … 'pent up on all sides both on this and the other side of the river, with tradesmen's and dyers' houses, who foul the water by their constant washing and cleaning their cloth'.

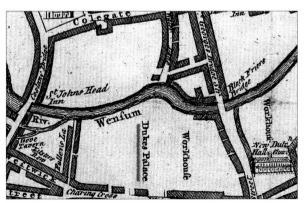
Duke's Palace on Samuel King's map of 1766

Duke St Bridge at Castle Mall

Stark, the Norwich School artist, drew the site of his father's dyeworks adjacent to the cast-iron bridge with its characteristic design of three decreasing circles. Stark Senior was a master craftsman who could dye bombazine fabric the deep black required for Victorian mourning. He also developed a method for staining the silk warp the exact same shade of red as the wool weft, thus producing the famous Norwich Red shawls. This involved madder, a tin mordant and the fortuitously chalky waters of the Wensum, yielding a deep, true scarlet. There were reports that the river would sometimes turn scarlet and it seems safe to assume that it was Stark who did this when he emptied his dye vats.

Soane's bridge on St George's Street

From the Duke Street Bridge it is possible to peer downstream to see the next crossing, a far more elegant affair. This is the St George's/Blackfriars' Bridge, which was built of Portland stone by Sir John Soane (1783-4) before he became Surveyor of the Bank of England. There is, however, no direct route for the riverside walker. Instead, you could skip a block by turning right, up Duke Street and past the Electric Company's buildings by Boardman, or you could do as I did and turn left down Duke Street then right along Colegate. This more pictureque diversion takes you past Howlett

and White's Norvic shoe factory built by Edward Boardman in 1876 and 1895. Around the end of the nineteenth century it was the largest shoe factory in the country. Although large, it employed a fraction of the outworkers employed in the textile trade that had sustained the city in previous centuries.

I reconnected with the riverside by turning right up St George's Street, crossing St George's Green and following the river via the north bank. But to get to Fye Bridge requires a lateral arabesque through Friars Quay, a residential development built on Jewson's Victorian timber yard. This 1970s housing has assimilated well despite Pevsner and Wilson's deathless judgement, 'It falls only just short of being memorable'. Then to the bridge. The first recorded crossing here dates from the middle of the twelfth century although excavations in 1896 suggested this was predated by a wooden walkway that connected the Tombland side to the Anglo-Scandinavian settlement in Norwich-over-the-Water. The present bridge, whose double arches are based on downstream Bishop Bridge, was built in 1933.

Crossing to the south bank, I left Norwich-over-the-Water, walking along the attractive Quayside until I came to Whitefriars. There was a wooden bridge here as far back as 1106 but what was then known as St Martin's Bridge was destroyed by the Earl of Warwick when he tried to deny Robert Kett's rebels access to the city during Kett's Rebellion of 1549. In 1591 this was replaced by a stone bridge that survived until the City Engineer constructed the present Whitefriars Bridge in 1924 -1925.

For a variety of reasons – some geographical, some political – the Norwich weavers were slow to address competition from the north and their eventual riposte is visible from the bridge. This was St James Mill, built by the Norwich Yarn Company (1836-9) to accommodate power looms. On the third floor, Willett & Nephew had 50 such machines that were able to produce more of

Fye Bridge

Whitefriars Bridge with St James Mill behind

the famous 'Norwich Red' shawls than would have been possible using traditional hand looms in outworkers' lofts. However, by the time the company began production in 1839, the huge factories in Yorkshire and Paisley were already mass-producing shawls. St James Mill is therefore a memorial to the demise of the weaving industry that for centuries had underpinned the city's status as second city. Still, the architectural commentator Ian Nairn, who was normally stinting in his praise of Norwich, thought this *the noblest of all English Industrial Revolution Mills.'*

Just beyond Whitefriars' Bridge is a bend in the river that now cradles the Magistrate's and the County Courts but in 1825 this was the site of the St Martin's Gasworks that supplied public lighting. Initially, this was fuelled by whale oil that illuminated the marketplace and Surrey Street but five years later it was converted to burn coal. During the balloon mania of the early 1800s, coal gas – which was lighter than air – was used to lift balloons more efficiently than hot air. From this site, the balloons would be inflated and led to nearby ascension sites, such as the Cavalry Barracks on Barrack Street across the water. In 1839 it is recorded that balloonists used parachutes to drop a monkey in a basket over Mousehold Heath and a cat over Catton.

At the next bend the river turns through ninety degrees to run south, defending this side of the city unaided by a city wall until it reconnects with the built defences at the end of this journey at Carrow. The fifty-foot-high Cow Tower (rebuilt late fourteenth century) was strategically placed here because of the perceived threat from the higher ground across the river. It is an early example of Norwich brickwork into which, for nine shillings each, stonemason Snape inserted cross-loops to accommodate longbows, crossbows or hand-held artillery. Through the tower's barred gate it is possible to see the tapered embrasures that allowed a wide range of fire. Still, this redoubtable-looking structure didn't deter Robert Kett's men during their righteous uprising against land

The John Jarrold bridge

Cow Tower

Walking along the south side of the river, the next bridge after Whitefriars' is the curving J shape of the John Jarrold Bridge of 2011. This box girder, clad in weathered steel with a hardwood deck, seems to me to be the most welcoming of the later bridges. It connects the cathedral precinct and the thirteenth century Adam and Eve pub with the St James Place Business Quarter and to Mousehold Heath beyond.

enclosures for in 1549 their master-gunner fired down from Kett's Heights, damaging the battlements.

Around the bend, the riverside presents a scene of deceptive tranquility – a perfect English setting with Norwich School's cricket field setting the stage for the Norman Cathedral in the background. But in 1549 this is where the city's guns returned fire upon the rebels commanding the heights at the edge of Mousehold

Bishop Bridge

they would be drawn into battle, overwhelmed, and their ringleaders hanged. But when looking across to the Lollards Pit pub it is impossible not to spare a further thought for the earlier followers of John Wycliffe (d.1384) who were taken over this bridge to their place of execution. Before the Protestant Reformation, Wycliffe – an early critic of the pomp and wealth of the Catholic Church – believed that the scriptures, not man-made ceremony, provided the only way to understand the word of God. He himself died of a heart attack but those of his followers who refused to recant were burnt at the stake as heretics. Wycliffe's adherents, the Lollards, worshipped by reading the scriptures and it may have been their habit of reading aloud that gave them their name, after the Old Dutch word for muttering.

Heath. A little further downstream the rebel guns, which had been captured from the king's forces, fired down upon what was then a fortified Bishop Bridge. In reduced form it survives as our only medieval bridge (c 1340).

Whenever I stand on Bishop Bridge I think of Kett's men streaming across to take the city for a brief interlude before they retreated to their encampment; from there

The next stopping place on the riverside walk is at Pull's Ferry, a name that now seems to apply to both the fifteenth century watergate and the seventeenth century ferry house alongside it. The watergate no longer offers a waterway into the cathedral, for it was filled-in about 1780, but when building started on the cathedral in 1096

Pull's Ferry

Foundry Bridge

Station was constructed on the eastern bank of the Wensum and the original wooden bridge was replaced by an iron structure. To form a better connection between the station and the city centre with its agricultural markets, Prince of Wales Road (1850s/1860s) was built as a wide, sweeping avenue based on rubble from the old city wall at Chapelfield. And in 1888, Foundry Bridge was made correspondingly wider, forming a direct route along which animals could be driven from the station to various stock markets around the foot of the Castle.

To continue the walk interrupted by Foundry Bridge, do not do as I did and follow the seductive arrow on the side of Norwich Nelson Premier Inn for it leads to a dead end. And don't plough on up Prince of Wales Road since – diverting as it is – this takes you too far from the river. Instead, switch to the station side of the river where the contrast between now and then couldn't be more stark: modern leisure versus Victorian industry. From 1999 the Riverside leisure complex – consisting of gym, cinema, bowling, pub, restaurants – replaced the enormous Riverside Works of engineers Boulton and Paul, which began as a Victorian enterprise on the opposite bank.

the open channel allowed building stone to be conveyed right up to the mason's yard. The cathedral was made from local rubble faced with either Barnack stone from near Stamford or a lighter, smoother Caen stone from Normandy. In a prodigious logistical exercise, the Normans brought every piece of Caen stone across the Channel and up this waterway.

The ferry house wasn't always known as Pull's Ferry for on his Norwich Plan of 1807, Cole referred to it as Sandling's Ferry. In the seventeenth century, Sandling (elsewhere, Sandlin) plied a ferry boat here but when Cole drew his map the ferry was being run by John Pull, who was active from 1796 to 1841. Despite the proximity of toll-free Bishop Bridge, the ferry operators somehow managed to make a living.

The riverside walk continues along the city-side bank until you have no option but to emerge onto the road bridge via steps adjacent to the Compleat Angler pub on prince of Wales Road. This is Foundry Bridge of 1811, which takes its name from a former ironworks, signalling our entry into a former industrial quarter after the present-day quietness of the cathedral precincts. The first bridge between the city and the Thorpe side was a wooden toll bridge. Then in 1844, when the railway arrived from Great Yarmouth, Thorpe

Boulton & Paul's Riverside Works c1983. ©Mike Page

Like their great rivals Barnard Bishop and Barnards several bridges upstream, Boulton and Paul produced wire netting amongst an enormous range of products for farm, estate and garden. During World War I they were asked by the government to turn to war production and the company began a distinguished record of manufacturing planes that flew from their aerodrome on Mousehold Heath. They made more Sopwith Camels (Snoopy's biplane of choice) than any other company but they also produced planes to their own design. Not for them the terror-inducing names like 'Typhoon', 'Thunderbolt' or 'Spitfire' but light bombers named after the amiable Norfolk seaside villages, Sidestrand and Overstrand, and a night-fighter named for that well-camouflaged bird of the Norfolk Broads, the Bittern.

When I took this walk in 2018 it was impossible to avoid the seething activity on the other side of the river where the newly-coined 'St Anne's Quarter' was under construction. Looking across to the rear of this large building site I could just make out Howard House, a historic building that was propped up for so many years that the scaffolding was said to have gained listed status. The Howards, of course, were the Dukes of Norfolk whose abandoned waterlogged palace cropped up in the first part of the walk, on the opposite side of the city. Howard House was built in 1660 by Henry, 6th Duke of Norfolk, on land seized by King Henry VIII from the Austin Friars. Here, John Evelyn laid out for the duke a pleasure garden that was still marked on eighteenth century maps as 'My Lord's Garden'. There is nothing in this ducal connection to explain the name of the new 'quarter' although the 1884 Ordnance Survey map provides clues. St Ann's Works, where the Smithdales cast the iron required for their business as millwrights, was named for St Ann's Chapel that once

Novisad Bridge

stood here. The former foundry is just part of a larger site that envelopes part of the Old Brewery on King Street, several maltings and the only Synagogue Street in the country (bombed in WWII).

Since 2009 it has been possible to cross back to the city side via the Lady Julian Bridge named for Julian of Norwich, the anchoress (c1342-c1416) whose Revelations of Divine Love is said to be the first English book written by a woman. If you were to cross her bridge, turn left on King Street then right on St Julian's Alley you would come to her eponymous Anglo-Norman church and the cell in which she was immured, all largely rebuilt after the Blitz.

The Lady Julian Bridge is a swing bridge that can allow masted ships through to the widened bend immediately to the north. This dogleg in the river is the turning basin that marks the head of navigation for large ships for only pleasure boats are small enough to pass beneath Foundry Bridge. However, by the time this bridge was

built in the early twentieth century, Norwich was no longer an active port; river commerce had dropped off significantly by the 1970s and by the following decade was all but dead.

On the city side of the river, ships returning to Great Yarmouth would have passed along the ancient wharves where medieval merchants like Robert Toppes sent their cloth for export and where grain was unloaded for the maltings that supplied the large Norwich breweries along King Street.

Now, on the stretch up to Carrow Bridge, riverside apartment-blocks dominate both sides of the river. Joining the two is the Novi Sad Friendship Bridge , built by May Gurney (2001) to mark the twinning of Norwich with the Serbian city. It also links commuters living in the city-side apartments to the railway station. One of the most prominent apartment blocks is a redbrick building, a former flour mill that started life in 1837 as the Albion Yarn Mill. Earlier, we came across St James'

Mill near Whitefriars' Bridge, built about the same time to house power looms in a vain attempt to revive our failing textile trade. It seems likely that the Albion Yarn Mill made silk and mohair thread to be used in our weaving industry upstream but trade was already in a terminal decline and by the 1870s the Albion Yarn Mill was being used as a confectionery works.

The final pedestrian bridge inside the old city walls is Carrow Bridge. In order for seagoing ships to visit those wharves at the back of King Street the central section of this bascule bridge would have to have been raised, temporarily halting the traffic that flows past the football stadium on Carrow Road. In still earlier times, a barrier to entry was provided by the paired boom towers on the south side of Carrow Bridge, part of the early fourteenth-century defensive ring. Boom towers lowered a boom or a beam across the river so

The red-brick buildings of the Albion Yarn (later, Flour) Mill

that tolls could be extracted from shipping but, in this case, a chain of Spanish iron was raised or lowered by a windlass in the tower on the city side.

This two-part walk around the river underlines the richness of the city's industrial past. Once, Norwich made things. Its pre-eminent textile trade lingered on into the nineteenth century to be replaced by a variety of trades of the Industrial Revolution: shoe-making, iron-working, brewing, brush-making, general engineering and other light manufacturing industries, many of them near the river. But during the later stages of this riverside walk there was little to show of those old trades since all traces of productive industry have been erased in favour of housing and leisure. The journey stopped at the last road bridge, just short of Colman's mustard factory that was synonymous with this city for a century and half, but when I wrote the blog post the factory was due to close and the future of the site was unclear.

Carrow Bridge opening in 1964 ©georgeplunkett.co.uk

The defensive boom towers with Carrow Bridge in the background. Courtesy broadlandmemories.co.uk

It's always safer writing about things like buildings that have stood the test of time than ephemera that could be winnowed away with the next economic downturn but when I first started writing my blog I wrote a short post on lampshades.

The outsize lampshades in Pizza Express in the Norwich Forum were decorated with molecular models of the four DNA bases that are sufficient to make the entire genetic code – a surprising choice for a fast food restaurant. The penny dropped when I saw these models repeated around an image of Sir Paul Nurse, the city's own Nobel Prize-winner. Paul had devoted his career to the study of yeast genetics and this explained the connection between yeast and pizza dough. But there are many kinds of yeast and Paul Nurse worked on fission yeast (where the mother cell divides by building a new wall across its middle), not on baker's yeast used for making pizza dough (where the mother cell pops out a bud in order to make a daughter).

So that cells don't get smaller and smaller with each division they normally devote time to doubling in size before the mechanism is triggered to make them divide again. Grow and divide, grow and divide. Paul had been studying a mutant form of fission yeast that divided prematurely, before they had time to grow back to the mother's size; so instead of maintaining average family size the daughters did become increasingly smaller. His initial research was carried out in Edinburgh where the tiny mutant was wryly called wee2. The mutated gene turned out to be responsible for the timing (or in the mutant's case, the mistiming) of cell division. This was essentially the same gene that Leland Hartwell in the States had identified as a controller of division in budding yeast. But although the two mechanisms by which these two kinds of yeast divide are different in detail (budding vs splitting) they share essentially the same gene involved in triggering the act of division.

And in one of those serendipitous connections by which science lurches forward, British scientist Tim Hunt,

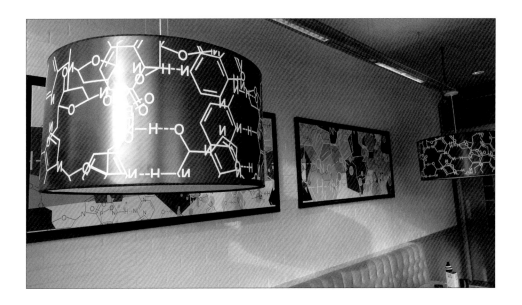

Sir Paul Nurse. Courtesy of Pizza Express

working on sea urchins, had identified a protein that accumulated just before their eggs divided, then disappeared after the split. Along with the Nurse/Hartwell proteins, Hunt's protein turned out to be a part of the complex that controls the timing of cell division. This 'master switch' is more or less identical in all living things – from yeast to plants to man – and when it goes wrong it can lead to the uncontrolled division of cancer cells. For this discovery, Paul Nurse, Tim Hunt and Leland Hartwell shared the 2001 Nobel Prize for Physiology and Medicine three ways.

All credit to Pizza Express for choosing this theme for a pizza restaurant.

Maps help us understand how we relate to the world. We have a fundamental sense of place that turns out to be hard-wired for there may actually be a mental map composed of a grid-like arrangement of filamentous cells in the brain. And as we learn, the map changes. If the hippocampus of a London taxi driver's brain can grow by 'doing the knowledge' and learning the best routes around London, imagine what happens to Norwich residents over a lifetime of following byzantine routes around medieval streets.

Although the old Roman road forded the Wensum around what is now Fye Bridge the Romans never settled here but passed on through to Venta Icenorum, their camp at Caistor (St Edmund). 'Proto-Norwich' was an Anglo-Saxon settlement based around Fye Bridge. By the early tenth century it was sufficiently established to be able to mint coins that bore the name of the Anglo-Saxon king on one side and on the other side was the place name 'Northwic', which establishes the location of that settlement on the north bank of the river. Although the Anglo-Saxons had been living peacefully with the Scandinavian invaders, King Sweyn of Denmark torched the town in 1004 in retribution for Æthelred the Unready's slaughter of resident Danes in the St Brice's Day massacre. But by the time of the Norman Conquest the settlement was aligned on a north-south axis with evidence of building on both sides of the River Wensum, including a marketplace on Tombland.

When the Normans arrived they imported Norman stone to build their monumental Cathedral and Castle, both considerably larger and more awe-inspiring than the predominantly wooden buildings of their predecessors. Importantly, these symbols of domination were located on the other side of the river and so Northwic gave way to the south. As part of this realignment, the Anglo-Scandinavian marketplace was transferred from Tombland to its present position

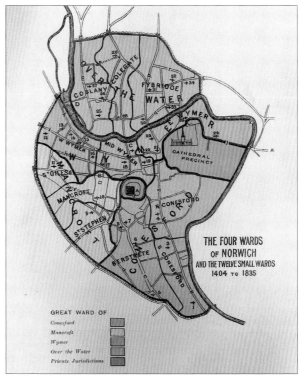

Norwich wards 1404-1835. From Hudson & Tingey (1906)
The Records of the City of Norwich.

under the gaze of the castle, from where the new French Borough extended westwards. Although the centre of gravity had shifted, the old Anglo-Scandinavian settlement on the north side of the river was still an important part of the Old Borough and, indeed, 'Norwich-over-the-Water' remained one of the city's four wards until the electoral reforms of the early nineteenth century.

The shape of the city inside a loop of the Wensum was literally set in stone by the building of the city walls. This took place from about 1294 to the middle of the following century, enclosing an administrative area

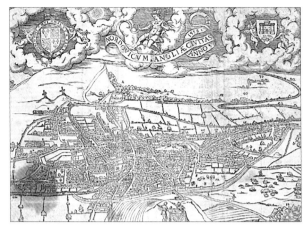

William Cuningham's map of Norwich 1558. Courtesy of British Library

larger than the City of London. The walls were built for the city's protection at a time when the country was at war with France but they also served the civil function of controlling the passage of taxable goods through the 12 city gates.

'Norwich', however, was not simply the area within its defensive bounds for the 1556 charter of Queen Mary I of England and Philip II of Spain specified that the hamlets of Earlham, Eaton, Catton, Thorpe, Trowse Millgate and Lakenham should be considered to be within the city's wider boundary.

The first authentic map of Norwich was made in 1558 by William Cuningham, a citizen of Norwich. It is notable for being the earliest surviving printed map of

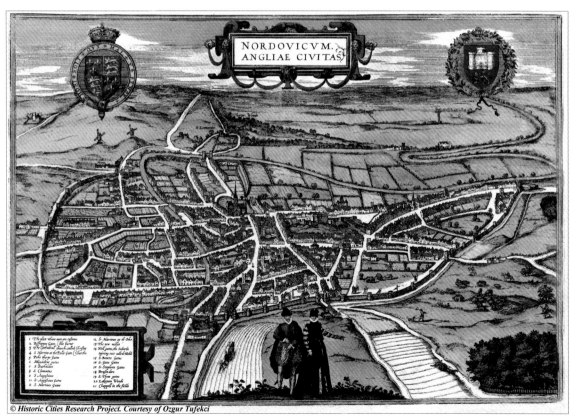

© Historic Cities Research Project. Courtesy of Ozgur Tufekci

Braun and Hogenberg's map of Norwich 1581. ©Historic Cities Research Project

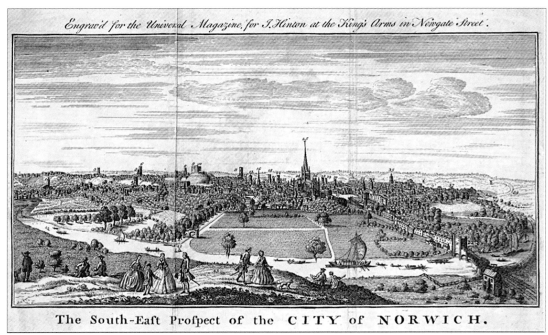

The South-Eaft Profpect of the CITY of NORWICH.

South-east prospect of the City of Norwich 1741 by Samuel and Nathaniel Buck. Courtesy Sanders of Oxford.

any English town or city outside London. The word 'civitas' on the banner recognises the city's proud status as a self-governing body. In 1404, the second charter from King Henry IV proclaimed that the city should be considered a county in its own right, separate from the county of Norfolk. The words, The County of the City of Norwich, appeared on maps until the local government reorganisation of 1974. Cuningham's map seems to counter perspective by tilting the distant ground towards us without quite providing the bird's eye view that would allow us to float above the city and look down upon it in scale. 'Prospects' like this could therefore be taken from a viewpoint outside the city; here, the cartographers at the lower edge seem to be pointing across to the windmills on Mousehold Heath.

Cuningham's map was to provide the model for most of the maps over the next 150 years. This included Georg

Braun and Franz Hogenburg's plan of 1581, even reproducing the archers practicing in Chapelfield. On the reverse was a poem delivered to Queen Elizabeth I during her visit to the city in 1578. The poem refers to 'Belgic friends': that is, the Strangers recently arrived from The Low Countries who were to revitalise our weaving industry. As late as 1676, Cuningham was still being imitated as evidenced by John Speed's map of Norfolk that still included the archers of a bygone age. The two prospects by Samuel and Nathaniel Buck, one from the south-east one from the north-east, show the city in the mid-eighteenth century when the city walls were still largely standing. Notice how much unbuilt space was present, something that Daniel Defoe recorded when he made his tour of the country 1724-1726:

"The walls of this city are reckoned three miles in circumference, taking in more ground than the city of

London; but much of that ground lying open in pasture-fields and gardens; nor does it seem to be, like some ancient places, a decayed declining town'.

It wasn't until 1696 that the professional surveyor Thomas Cleer broke away from Cuningham's template. His plan of Norwich did provide a bird's eye view and, more importantly, was the first to be printed to scale.

While Cuningham's map showed that one man's work could inspire generations of cartographers, others could turn to outright plagiarism, as occurred to land surveyor James Corbridge. In 1727, Corbridge published a fine plan of the city. Subscribers paid two shillings down

and three on delivery, while anyone wanting their house or arms to appear in the margins had to pay seven shillings down and three on delivery. For his next venture he advertised for subscriptions to allow him to make a new full-scale survey of Norfolk but, before the county map could emerge, two Norwich booksellers, William Chase and Thomas Goddard, planned to undercut him with a pirated version. To cast doubt on Corbridge's work the booksellers got one of his employees – the improbably named Thermometer Elinett – to send a letter to the local paper stating, incorrectly, that the new map would be a copy of previous maps with all their imperfections. Corbridge's reply in a rival paper settled the matter, accusing Elinett of not knowing the 'South End of the Needle for the North.'

With the exception of the small suburbs of Heigham and Pockthorpe, there was little development of Norwich beyond the city walls until the late eighteenth century. When the walls and gates were pulled down – and much of the old city walls bordering Chapelfield now lie beneath Prince of Wales Road – development did begin to creep outwards. But as the 1842 Heigham tithe map shows, there was still much open land immediately beyond the city walls, including fields and market gardens .

This was just before the sale of Unthank's and Steward's land holdings that, as I described in Colonel Unthank and the Golden Triangle, triggered the explosion in terraced-house building across Heigham. A new form of mass transport was required to convey workers from the expanding suburbs into the city centre where much of its industry was still concentrated. Between 1900 and 1935, the Norwich Electric Tramways, with its hub at Orford Place, provided routes around the city using electricity generated by the power station on Duke Street . Streets that for centuries had been negotiated by horse and cart were now unsuitable for unwieldy

1842 Heigham tithe map. Courtesy of Norfolk Record Office NRO BR276/1/0051. Open Government Licence.

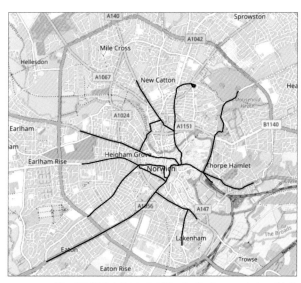

Norwich Electric Tramways Map. Creative Commons, Andrew Abbott.

trams and many old buildings had to be demolished before tramlines could extend into the suburbs. In 1933 the Eastern Counties Omnibus Company bought the tramways with the view to replacing them with petrol-driven buses.

In retaliation for the RAF bombing Lübeck in March 1942, the Luftwaffe announced they would bomb every English city with three stars in Baedeker's Travel Guide. These cities were to include Norwich, York, Bath, Exeter and Canterbury – all of cultural and historical importance. Norwich suffered badly in the 1942 Baedeker Raids. In the raid of April 1942, 258 people died and 784 were injured. The six-foot-square Norwich Bomb Map, now restored at the Norfolk Record Office, recorded 679 bombs that fell on the city between 1940 and 1945.

Just as the war was ending, the City Engineer HC Rowley – together with consultants CH James and S Rowland Pierce who had recently designed Norwich City Hall (1938) – were preparing the new City of

Norwich Plan. In this, they took a fresh look at the flow of traffic around the bomb-damaged centre. Once more, buildings were destroyed – this time in peace – streets were widened and the outline of a medieval city shaped like a leg of mutton was redefined for the convenience of the car.

Over the years the confines of Norwich have relaxed, in stages. In the nineteenth and early twentieth centuries, private (and later public) housing colonised the area between the breached city wall and what was to become the outer ring road. Until the 1920s there was little development beyond this and maps still showed much open land west of Colman Road and around the newly-

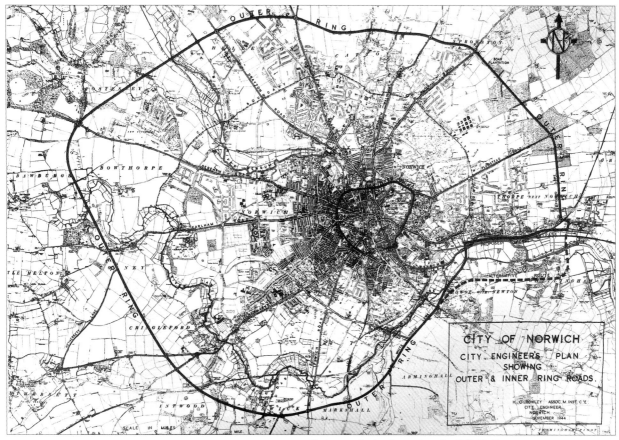

The inner and outer ring roads on the 1945 City Plan. Courtesy Norfolk Record Office.

completed Eaton Park. An Ordnance Survey map from 1928 shows that Christchurch Road, which connected Unthank Road to Earlham Road, had yet to be built on Church Commissioners' land but by the time this road was completed in 1935 the Colman Road stretch of the ring road was able to perform this function itself. Now, getting on for a century later, we have the Southern Bypass that together with the Northern Distributor Road almost encircles us. And as each new circle moves outwards like a ripple in a pond so the enclosed rural land succumbs to development.

I'd always been curious about the nether reaches of Norwich-over-the-Water, especially the historic Gildencroft area clinging on amongst the after effects of postwar modernisation. To visit my daughter in the north of the city I would drive through these streets, seeing them from a driver's perspective but, after discussing psychogeography with her, I promised to see this area in a slower, more reflective way.

There was a time you were free to imagine yourself a nineteenth century flâneur like Baudelaire, cane in hand, strolling the boulevards without a care. But ever since mid-twentieth century psychogeographers like Guy Debord stuck their oar in, with their socio-political ideas about the effects of environment on the pedestrian's psyche, the informed pedestrian has become sensitive to the buildings around them, especially on the urban fringes where awful things happen in the name of progress.

In his book, *Psychogeography*, Will Self wrote about walking to Manhattan from his house in south London (but not, I think, over the water) in order to regain 'the Empty Quarters', the hinterlands around airports. And in his 'alternative cartography' around the M25 London Orbital, Iain Sinclair famously wrote about walking through urban no-man's land. Other twenty-first century urban walkers – the new psychogeographers – suggest taking a playful approach to the exploration of the built environment, employing a variety of tricks to nudge the pedestrian off the beaten path in order to make them more aware of the urban landscape. Rob Macfarlane recommended following the path drawn on a map by an upturned tumbler while others throw dice at each intersection. Some perform 'ambulant signmaking' by following a letter traced on a map; one urban runner even used the GPS tracker in his running shoe to race around the streets, geotracking the outline of his privy member on the map. Hmm. This may be why Lauren Elkin, in her book *Flâneuse*, wrote about the need for female walkers to reclaim the streets. Me? I just walked against the flow of traffic towards the Norman marketplace, deliberately dawdling, taking in the disastrous effects of postwar development.

I started my walk towards the city, not where the old north gate of St Augustine's once stood at the top of St Augustine's Street, but by taking a closer look at a building I'd often glimpsed from my car. This was on Starling Road, off Magpie Road, just outside the old city wall. The building is a relic of the once thriving Norwich shoe industry that, like much of the city's trade, took place here in Norwich-over-the-water *(Ultra Aquam)*. The concrete lettering on the parapet reads: The British United Shoe Machinery Co Ltd 1925. This Leicester firm used to make equipment for the Norwich shoemakers but collapsed in 2000. When I wrote my blog post in 2017 the building was occupied by the printers, Gallpen. Gallpen offers a fine example of nominative determinism (my geometry master really was called Mr Angle) since oak galls were once used in manufacturing ink. In a Jarrold's trade book from 1910 the founder, Charles Gaunt Gallpen (b 1859), advertised himself as a printer, with the unintentionally ominous slogan: *"Call on me or I will call on you."*

Gallpen Printers on Starling Road. Derelict when revisited in 2020

Tower and part of City Wall revealed by demolition of a print shop

Next, I crossed busy Magpie Road, walking west towards a flint tower and a segment of the medieval city wall revealed when Magpie Printers was demolished in 2013. To follow the wall westwards I crossed the junction on St Augustine's Street to see the wall re-emerge on a tract of land between Bakers Road and St Martin's-at-Oak Wall Lane. On the outer side of the vestigial wall is a green sward covering what was once the external ditch).

On the city side of the wall was a tract of land known as the Jousting Acre. Here, men-at-arms practiced jousting

The City Wall and the former City Ditch

with lances and – as was compulsory in the medieval period – young men would have performed their archery practice with bows or crossbows. In his History of Norwich, Francis Blomefield mentions: *'In the 15th year of his reign, the King appointed a turnament to be held at Norwich.'* Local historian Stuart McLaren suggests that King Edward III probably saw the tournament at the Jousting Acre in February 1340.

Georgian doorway in Sussex Street

Walking down St Augustine's Street the first turning is into Sussex Street, an attractive road containing Georgian terraces. Dating mainly to 1821-1824 these were built for the respectable working/lower middle class. Number 22 is more genteel, its door flanked by fluted Doric columns topped with a segmental fanlight. Opposite, a similar doorcase decorates No 21, which forms part of a terrace of three-storeyed houses. Adjacent to this is a 1971 conversion to flats by Edward Skipper and Associates. Tucked away behind these houses is a modern development, Quintain Mews, whose name commemorates the revolving target used for practicing jousting: when hit with lance or sword it would swing around to sandbag the combatant.

The street is not as it would have been before the war although the modern intrusions have been done with sensitivity. On the south side of Sussex Street is the entry to 42 modern, split-level dwellings – The Lathes – owned by Broadland Housing Association. This development was built in 1976 by the architects Teather and Walls ('Associate for Edward Skipper and Associates'). The word 'lathes' is dialect for a grain barn and acknowledges the farm that once stood in this area. According to Blomefield, the farm belonged at various times to Sir John Paston, and two Shakespearean heroes: Sir John Fastolff of Caister (Falstaff is mentioned in five plays) and *'brave Sir Thomas Erpingham'* (Henry V) whose statue kneels above the Erpingham Gate of Norwich Cathedral.

Historically and architecturally St Augustine's is a fascinating street but the temptation to flit between its two sides is inhibited by the volume of traffic flowing out of the city from the inner ring road. St Augustine's would spring back to life if pedestrianised. Still, at the time of writing, the traffic hadn't put off young potters and artists who were adopting the street, some with pop-up galleries. For example, numbers 23 and 25 – with a combined range of five upper gables

– appeared to have been recently renovated, looking attractive in their new blue livery.

A cyclist who came into view as I was taking a photograph of number 33 provided further evidence of renewal for this was his house and he proudly mentioned he had just renovated his lucam, the oversized roof gables that seem to be typical of Norwich. Lucams provided extra height and lighting for the families – almost certainly some of the city's 'Strangers' – who would have worked at their handlooms at the peak of the city's woollen trade. Lucams are prominent on the east side of the street as are the cast-iron signs for various yards: Hindes Yard, Nichols Yard, Winecoopers Arms Yard and Rose Yard.

The influx of religious refugees from the Spanish Netherlands in the Elizabethan era created a demand for housing. This was met by squeezing poorly-built, insanitary 'yards' or 'courts' into the courtyards of larger properties fronting the streets. Rose Yard – the site of the ancient Rose Inn that once refreshed those

A gallery of five gables

The insanitary Rose Yard was behind the Rose Inn. ©georgeplunkett.co.uk

Lucams or weavers' windows

I passed a small building, now a children's nursery, that was built by the Society of Friends at the end of the seventeenth century then rebuilt after the original was destroyed in the 1942 Baedeker air raids. Nearby are the gates to the burial ground. These were open when I sought Amelia Opie's grave in the spring of 2017 but were locked later that year (and still locked in 2020) due to drink, drugs and dog poo.

I completed my stroll around Gildencroft by walking through St Crispin's Car Park and hopping up a bank to St Crispin's Road with its busy roundabout. Not wishing to play chicken with the heavy traffic I trekked back up Pitt Street (commemorating not Prime Minister Pitt but a rubbish pit) to find a safe crossing. And it was here, facing Sovereign House, that I was confronted by

attending jousting tournaments – accommodated 70 houses before they were demolished in the 1950s. For 50 of those slum dwellings the only source of water was the public pump in St Augustine's churchyard. A report from 1851 confirmed the awfulness: *'at the bottom is a large pool of nightsoil 15 feet by 25 feet from about 40 houses.'* Opposite Rose Yard is St Augustine's Church (late 1600s) whose parishioners are known as Red Steeplers on account of it being the only red-brick church-tower in the city. In the churchyard is the tomb of Thomas Clabburn (d.1858) who employed several hundred Norwich weavers. Clabburn produced silk and wool shawls that were responsible for a brief revival in the city's weaving trade in the mid-Victorian era. His efforts were appreciated for he is memorialised in the nave of the church by a marble monument funded by 600 Norwich weavers. A mulberry tree – a reminder of the silk yarn used in his shawls – stands next to his grave. Neighbouring the southern perimeter of the churchyard is Church Alley (1580), believed to be the longest row of Tudor houses in England. This leads to the wonderfully named street, Gildencroft, which commemorates an area that once roughly overlapped St Augustine's parish. Gildencroft is also the name of the small park I circumnavigated in search of the Quaker Burial Ground.

Grave of Thomas Clabburn, shawl-maker, in St Augustine's Church

The derelict Sovereign House, part of the Anglia Square development

the source of my irritation – Anglia Square and the ring road. Gildencroft had already been assured a peripheral presence by its location over the river *(Norwich Ultra Aquam)* but then, in the 1960s and 70s, the inner ring road severed ancient routes and consigned this area to an even more distant orbit: Norwich-over-the-ring-road *(Norwich Ultra Via Anulum)*.

In the decades after the war it must have seemed like a good thing to replace a bomb-damaged area of insanitary medieval housing with a flagship Brutalist office block that housed Her Majesty's Stationery Office and the city's own symbol of 60s modernity – the pedestrian precinct. But, in the case of HMSO at Sovereign House, modernity barely survived 50 years, and the shopping centre fails to thrive in a development that was never fully completed. This can't be blamed on a dislike of Brutalism in the provinces for we only have to look at how well concrete works in Lasdun's greenfield site at UEA. More likely the problem stemmed from the imposition of an out-of-scale, unsympathetic development on an historic district. Now, in a frightening example of history repeating itself, it is proposed to replace Anglia Square with a 20-storey-high tower surrounded by 12-storey, high-density housing. (In late 2020 the Secretary of

St Crispin's underpass

State refused planning permission.) I tried to complete my journey to the city centre by walking beneath St Crispin's Flyover that leapfrogs (but still manages to blight) medieval Magdalen Street but found my way blocked by a private trailer depot. So I doubled back and escaped via the only route available to pedestrians aiming straight for the marketplace – St Crispin's underpass. Flâneurs and flâneuses seeking a portal into this historic area are unlikely to find a less welcoming entrance but do it, explore Gildencroft and help reconnect it to the city centre.

Continuing my walk from St Augustines to the marketplace I escaped Norwich-over-the-Ringroad via St Crispin's underpass and entered the former industrial area on the north bank of the River Wensum.

Through the underpass all was sweetness and light. I was still in Norwich-over-the-Water but at least it was away from the lowering presence of Anglia Square. Now, modern buildings were in scale, the old street pattern had largely survived and there was a better class of graffiti. Pevsner and Wilson described the more sympathetic renovation of this former industrial quarter as a *"welcome softening of approach since the late 1980s."*
Around the corner on St Georges Street is a symbol of this enlightenment: a pair of houses that were renovated in 1986 instead of being demolished. The house on the right, dated 1670, used to be to be the King's Head pub and gained two lucams in the restoration.

C17 buildings restored in the 1980s, Cavell House in the background

Forming a backdrop to these early buildings is an office block, Cavell House, which, as a postmodern building, kicked against the uniformity of modernism by including a variety of references, some of them playful. One of these references, the horizontal run of windows on the upper floor, resembles the long throughlight or weavers' windows once common in the city's Victorian

Sherwyn House. Victorian brush factory renovated as apartments in the 1990s

factories. Another reference appears above the window heads of Cavell House: segmental arches punctuated by keystones. This feature was borrowed from its neighbour, Sherwyn House, labelled on an 1885 map as a 'brush manufactory'. By 1983 the brush factory was derelict and was converted to apartments as part of Feilden and Mawson's 1992 Calvergate development.

Just beyond Sherwyn House, a U-turn up Cross Lane then a right into Golden Dog Lane brought me to a building I had seen from the other side of the flyover. The defiant Tudor-style chimneys and crow-step gable belonging to Doughty's Hospital, an almshouse founded in 1687 by William Doughty for 24 poor men and eight poor women. By the mid-nineteenth century only a sparse outline of the original building remained and it was rebuilt in 1869, explaining its Victorian appearance. Now it provides 57 sheltered flats for the elderly.

Doughty's almshouses

On entering the site, two cast-iron parish plates can be seen fixed to a wall. In the Georgian era, in the absence of detailed maps, such plates were the way of defining the boundaries of the parish and its social and legal responsibilities. The letters S stand for Saint Saviour's Magdalen Street, the fifteenth century church with the truncated tower now literally overshadowed by the flyover. The symbol between these letters represents the truncated stone cross that gave its name to the Stump Cross district based around the former junction of Magdalen and St Botolph's Street, much altered by the Anglia Square development.

Parish plate for St Saviours with symbol for Stump Cross

Retracing my steps into Cross Lane I looked down Calvert Street towards Colegate and the Norman castle beyond. On the left side are two Victorian red-brick terraces: one recording 'GH 1896' in Guntons' brick tiles, the other with a stone inscribed 'Thompson's Buildings 1859'. A resident told me these were once council houses, sold under the Right-to-Buy scheme.

On the opposite side of the cobbled street is a grander prospect – a reminder of the area's former prosperity.

Georgian houses in Calvert Street

and Norwich, once part of the Danelaw. The link is celebrated in a 'Viking Norwich' wall plaque stating that the street runs along an Anglo-Scandinavian defensive bank and ditch. This area was in the heart of the north wic before the Normans built their regional capital on the south side of the Wensum.

Returning to Cross Lane I entered Muspole Street via Alms Lane. It was from here that I saw the St George's Works building site with Howlett and White's Norvic-Kiltie shoe factory (1926) in the background. This was an adjunct to their huge Norvic shoe factory on St Georges Street that employed 1200 workers in 1909.

Former shoe factories off Colegate

Straight over Duke Street I entered St Mary's Plain, one of the city's 15 open spaces. Where other cities have squares Norwich has plains. 'Plein' is another borrowing from the sixteenth century Dutch and Flemish Protestant refugees who, fleeing Spanish Catholic persecution, settled here and reinvigorated our weaving trade. Adjacent to Zoar Strict and Particular Baptist Chapel is the former home of Thomas Pykerell, cloth merchant, sheriff and three times Mayor of Norwich in the fifteenth century. Pykerell's House is one of only six thatched buildings in the city. It was gutted by incendiary bombs in the 1940s and we are fortunate to have it in its restored state.

As our weaving industry declined so the boot and shoe manufacturing trade increased and here, in the plain, is a former giant shoe factory, part of what is now the stalled redevelopment of the 'Shoe Quarter'. The name of Sexton Son and Everard Ltd, which has been over-painted, sits on top of the building – the blacked-out lettering an unwitting reminder of the damage inflicted in the Blitz. The shoe factory that started in 1876 folded 100 years later.

Now for Duke Street, widened in 1972 to become a main feeder for the inner ring road as outlined in the 1945 City of Norwich Plan. Duke Street is named for the Duke of Norfolk's sixteenth century palace that once stood on the site part-occupied by the St Andrews Street car park. As I crossed the Duke Street bridge I left Norwich-over-the-Water behind. The original Duke's Palace Bridge of 1822 was an attractive cast-iron structure, replaced as part of the 1972 road-widening scheme. Its replacement is an unprepossessing bridge that blocks pedestrian movement along the river bank. Fortunately, the Norwich Society preserved the old bridge, which was later re-erected over the entrance to the Castle Mall car park.

A riverside gangway to the east of the present bridge provides a vantage point to look back over the river, across to the site of the large shoe factory that Edward Boardman designed for Howlett and White on St George's Plain. It has one of the last remaining chimney stacks in Norwich-over-the-Water; another one – in a district that once abounded in industrial chimneys – belongs to the Brush Factory, now Sherwyn House.

Sexton Son & Everard's shoe factory 1876-1976

Electricity Board buildings on the Duke St Bridge. Derelict since 1999

To the right of the Duke Street Bridge is a mostly derelict industrial complex that provided power for the city's first electric street lamps. In 1892 Boardman and Son designed the conversion of the old Duke's Palace Ironworks for the Norwich Electric Light Company but by the 1920s this was superseded by the power station at Thorpe and the Duke Street site was converted to offices.

Left into St Andrews Street then right into one of the very few post-medieval streets in the city: Exchange Street. Originally called Museum Street, then Post Office Street, it was renamed yet again after the opening of the Corn Exchange (1828). In 1832, Exchange Street finally connected through to St Andrews Street. This allowed beasts and wagons entering St Augustine's Gate in the north to be driven to market via the recently opened Duke Street Bridge. They would have passed the original corn exchange in Exchange Street, which was replaced in 1861 by a larger building that functioned well into the twentieth century. In 1963, however, the new corn exchange was itself demolished to make way for the extension to Jarrolds Department Store at the corner of Exchange Street and Bedford Street.

At last, the marketplace. The Anglo-Scandinavian market was based in Tombland but the entire axis of the city changed when the Normans built the castle in the late eleventh century and installed a market in

Exchange St Corn Exchange of 1861, site now part of Jarrolds Dept Store
©georgeplunkett.co.uk

its present position, outside the motte in the Mancroft district. Over recent years there had been too many unoccupied stalls in the ancient market but I noticed a revival of its fortunes due the city council's introduction of a 'Global Market' – pop-ups selling street food from around the world. Hybrid vigour comes to the rescue, as it has done throughout the long history of this city.

Norwich market with Guidhall in the distance

It was because of the very deep layer of chalk beneath this city that the historian Stefan Muthesius wrote that Norwich was further away from good building stone than any other place in England – we've already heard about the Normans importing their own stone from Caen in Normandy. Transporting stone over long distances required serious financial and logistical clout so when less wealthy builders of medieval Norwich needed something more grand than timber-framed buildings they turned to the flint that ran in seams through the subterranean chalk.

Noel Coward was able to raise a wan smile simply by getting Amanda in 'Private Lives' to say, 'Very flat, Norfolk.' It is dreadfully flat. When someone once showed me Beeston Bump in the distance – at 63 metres the highest point in the county – his arm barely flickered above the horizontal. This flatness derives from the county's sedimentary foundations, made from the skeletal remains of unimaginable numbers of marine organisms that rained down upon the flat seabed more than 60 to 95 million years ago.

These small, often microscopic, sea creatures had skeletal structures based on the chemical elements calcium and silicon. The calcium accounts for the chalk layers beneath us, the hardness of our drinking water that percolates through it, and the white deposits left overnight on our draining boards. Silicon is even less soluble than calcium. As marine animals burrowed through the Cretacean sludge at the bottom of the sea they created tunnels that somehow provided the right environment for the crystallisation of silicon salts into hard flint nodules. So the holes and branches that we admire in flint are a record of the journeys taken by marine animals through the ancient ooze.

In the 1930s, just down the coast from the Beeston Bump, Henry Moore, Barbara Hepworth and their spouses holidayed in Happisburgh. Here, they became deeply fascinated by the organic forms of the East Anglian flints that translated into the sculptural forms of their work. Hepworth is said to have created one of the first sculptures with a hole through it for non-representational purposes. And Moore – whose own sculptures were famously lumpy and bumpy – created a high-flown intellectual slogan out of the cavities created by Cretacean sea creatures: *"The hole connects one side with another, making it immediately more three-dimensional. A hole itself can have as much shape and meaning as a solid mass."*

On St George's Green, 'Sea Form (Atlantic) 1964' by Barbara Hepworth

Norfolk claims more than its fair share of round-towered churches. One idea is that these towers were a cultural import, brought here by the Anglo-Saxons who later used them as protection against the marauding Danes. However, perhaps twice as many round towers appear to be Norman. Our geology offers a more convincing explanation. While more than 120 round-tower Norfolk churches map on top of the East Anglian chalk bed, just fifty are found in wider East Anglia and virtually none further afield. If round towers were a cultural import why should they be restricted to such a small part of the country when the invaders themselves ventured further afield? The more mundane explanation seems the most likely one: that, in the absence of dressed stone to make decent corners (quoins), the seams of flint amongst the chalk were used for making round towers.

Flint is a difficult building material, expensive to knap into cubes and too small in section to make good, stable corner-stones. In the city of Norwich, wealthy patrons – like the Church – could afford to build square-sectioned towers with quoins made of imported stone and only a handful of the city's medieval churches are round-towered. Thirty-one of about 57 pre-Reformation churches survive, providing the basis for two tired tropes about Norwich: that it has the largest number of city towers north of the Alps (i.e., only Rome has more); and it had one church for every week of the year and enough pubs for every day of the year.

An example of a round tower in the city can be seen just off the west end of St Benedict's Street. The tower of St Benedict's church stands alone, orphaned by the German bomb that destroyed the main body of the church. This tower is made of knobbly, unknapped flint, bonded with lime mortar, the simplest way of building with this material.

Different ways of handling flint can be seen on the medieval Guildhal. In 1404 a royal charter granted the city the right of self-government and the Guildhall was built as an expression of local power and prestige.

The round tower of St Benedict's Church

North wall of Norwich Bridewell

Left, square-knapped flint. Norwich Guildhall. Right, irregularly-shaped fractured flints surrounded by galettes

For the west wall, flint pebbles were fractured with a hammer to expose the crystalline black interior. Such simply-knapped flints, faced on only one side and roughly circular in section, could not be laid in neat courses like bricks. Instead, the masons made a virtue out of necessity by filling the irregular gaps with flat flint chips inserted edgeways into the mortar. Apart from protecting the exposed mortar these galettes (French for wafer) swirled around the knapped flints to form flowing patterns that were decorative in their own right.

A neater, more expensive solution is also illustrated on the Guildhall where flint has been square-knapped with such skill that the cubes could be laid in regular courses without the visible need for mortar or galettes to fill the cracks. Competing with this for the prize of best flint wall in the city is the long north wall of the old Bridewell, now the Museum of Norwich. Indeed, it has been claimed to be the finest specimen of faced flintwork in the country. It is a magnificent wall although the individual flints are not as precisely squared as those on the east end of the Guildhall. As a consequence the rectangular flints are not in perfect courses but that is part of its beauty and you may love it the more for its imperfection.

Back to the east end of the Guildhall (rebuilt in the sixteenth century) where there is a good example of the way that ashlar (usually pale limestone) was used to introduce pattern into a flint wall. This is *flushwork*, in which flat, dressed stone forms a pattern on the same plane as the faced flint. In *proudwork*, the stone stands proud of the flint. At the Guildhall, black diamond shapes of square-knapped flint alternate with diamonds of pale limestone to form a chequerboard that alludes to the building's use as an exchequer where fees and fines were paid on a checkered cloth for counting money. There is another beautiful example on the Guildhall in King's Lynn.

Chequered flushwork on the east end of Norwich Guildhall

Glorious tracery flushwork on the east end of St Michael Coslany

Flushwork is found where flint is common. It was a speciality of Norfolk and Suffolk and was at its most inventive from the mid-fourteenth century during the Perpendicular Period. St Michael (or Miles) Coslany in Norwich-over-the-Water contains a famous example that was greatly admired by John Sell Cotman. On the restored east end, limestone set amongst the flint forms a pattern that mimics the stone ribs in the adjacent Perpendicular window; it is quite beautiful, making this one of the finest example of tracery flushwork anywhere.

Flushwork in Norwich can be dated with confidence back to at least 1316 when the citizens rebuilt the St Ethelbert's Gate in reparation for setting fire to it and other parts of the cathedral in 1272. What we see today is the result of William Wilkins' restoration of 1815, but the original pattern is recorded in old engravings. The flint and stone patterns on St Ethelbert's Gate take the form of flushwork wheels, reminiscent of a rose window. The armed man and the dragon carved in the stone spandrels below show St George in his traditional protective role at the threshold although the confrontation can't help but remind us of the thirteenth century conflict for which 30 rioting citizens were hanged.

The inventive use of stone and flint might be imagined to have died away when church-building declined after the Reformation. Indeed, in 1671 the diarist John Evelyn wrote that Sir Thomas Browne of Norwich had informed him that *'they had lost the art of squaring flints, in which they once excell'd, and of which the churches, best houses, and walls, are built ...'.* The magnificent restoration of the east wall of St Michael Coslany in the nineteenth century shows us that the late medieval skills weren't completely lost. And for perfectly squared flint go to St Andrew's Plain and look at the disused public lavatory – built in 1892.

'Rose window' flushwork on Norwich Cathedral's Ethelbert Gate

Perfectly squared flints on the defunct lavatory outside St Andrew's Hall

The front of Prospect House

Prospect House was constructed in 1968-70 for Eastern Counties Newspapers, owners of the Eastern Daily Press and Norwich Evening News. Built in the Brutalist style, with horizontal bands of ribbon-window sandwiched between layers of ribbed concrete, Prospect House invites military comparison for it belongs to the same family as the slit-bunker, dominating the hill on Cattlemarket Street as it levels off on Golden Ball Street

Enemies of Brutalism probably cheered on hearing that Prospect House failed to gain listed status in view of its 'modest architectural quality'. But what has always redeemed this building – which Pevsner and Wilson felt was made with a lack of conviction – is the facade, especially Bernard Meadows' 'Public Sculpture' at the entrance. Unlike the building itself the front has been listed by Heritage England. Meadows, who was to become President of the Norfolk Contemporary Art Society in the 1960s and 70s, came to prominence in the 1952 Venice Biennale when one of his sculptures provided the name for the Geometry of Fear School of young, post-war sculptors that included Lynn Chadwick and Eduardo Paolozzi.

As Henry Moore's first assistant, Bernard Meadows was no stranger to rounded sculptural forms pierced with holes – holes influenced by the holey pebbles that fascinated Moore and Barbara Hepworth on their holidays at Happisburgh on the Norfolk coast. As we saw in a previous chapter, the organic shapes of flint are thought to derive from the crystallisation of silica in the burrows formed by sea creatures in the ooze at the bottom of the Cretacean sea. Moore and his friends were probably unaware of the chemistry involved but the forms achieved by the hardening salts evidently had a formative effect on their art.

Meadows went on to become Professor of Sculpture at the Royal College of Art and in his own work explored smooth, rounded forms penetrated by voids. One influential piece was 'Help', consisting of two solid shapes crushing a bronze sphere, looking so much like a pliable dough-ball poked by a finger. He repeated this playful theme for his sculpture at Prospect House with large golden balls – again with deep indentations – crushed and oozing between blocks of concrete. The success of the sculpture is undoubtedly due to the

Princess Alexandra opening Prospect House 1970 ©Eastern Daily Press/Archant

Bernard Meadows' sculpture

larger context in which it is placed. The effect of rigid, linear seams of raw concrete on Prospect House is softened somewhat by the roundness of split pebbles – flint – that clad the lower floor and by the bank of uncoursed pebbles that connects the building with the street. Meadows' sculpture takes this a step further by reminding us that even rigid materials like organically-shaped flints and concrete were at one time liquid: even hard materials ooze.

In his work for Prospect House, the sculptor found the perfect place to refine his previous piece Help, in the process gaining a titter from the proximity to Golden Ball Street. Norwich-born Meadows would have known that the Golden Ball Inn once stood a hundred or so yards down the hill. He would also have been familiar with the adjacent Woolpack Inn, on Golden Ball Street,

The Woolpack Inn

whose sign hung there long before Prospect House was built. The sign is a gilded metal woolsack trussed so tightly it bulges between the strings – another playful allusion to the nature of materials.

(Based on a Tweet made by @ReggieUnthank on March 28th 2019)

Fire has been a potent force in shaping the townscape, especially when buildings were made of timber and thatch. In the period before the Conquest, near a low river crossing, a defended Anglo-Scandinavian settlement evolved on the north bank of the River Wensum. This was the *North Wic* whose name is recorded on coins minted there during the reign of the first English king, Athelstan (925-939). But in 1004 the Danish king, Sweyn Forkbeard, took vengeance for the death of his sister during the St Brice's Day Massacre by burning the northern settlement. As it says in The Anglo-Saxon Chronicles: *'This year came Sweyne with his fleet to Norwich, plundering and burning the whole town.'*

Vikings at the gates. Norwich City Hall. James Woodford 1938

Two 'lost' churches on the north bank, in the Magdalen Street area of Norwich, had suffixes referring to fire: St Mary's Unbrent (unburnt) and St Margaret's *in Combusto* or, *in Combusto Loco*. The qualifier, 'in combusto loco', identifies these churches as survivors

of a conflagration but by the Reformation both had disappeared. Whether the north *wic* was too devastated to be rebuilt as a regional capital, or whether the opposite bank offered greater opportunity for expansion and defence, the Norman invaders settled on the south side. With their prodigious cathedral adjacent to the old Anglo-Scandinavian marketplace on Tombland, and their castle overlooking the new market in the French Borough – both inspiring more awe than anything built by their predecessors – the Normans radically altered the layout of Norwich for the following millennium.

In August 1272 a quarrel erupted at the annual Tombland Fair over whether stall-holders should pay fees to the city or the priory. The prior's armed men claimed that the old marketplace outside the cathedral gates was under their jurisdiction, not the city's, and in the ensuing fight a citizen was killed by a crossbow. The belligerent prior, William de Brunham, fled to Yarmouth and returned with barges of armed men who *'fell upon citizens with fire and sword'*. While the priory men barred the monastery gates and fired crossbows at passing citizens, citizens on the tower of St George Tombland shot slings of fire that set the monastery ablaze, destroying much, including the library.

Tower of St George Tombland, in Princes Street, cathedral spire in the background

Site of the Popinjay Inn in Tombland (1962). ©www.georgeplunkett.co.uk

The first of the 1507 fires started on Easter Tuesday and devastated the city. Over four days, 718 buildings burned. The fire is said to have started at The Popinjay Inn on Tombland – the site now occupied by a modern building, currently occupied by All-Bar-One.

The second fire started on Ascension Day 1507 in the house of a French surgeon in the Colegate area. It raged for two days and a night, destroying a further 360 houses. Stone-built churches survived but very few timber-framed and thatched houses did. Almost half the city's houses were destroyed. Sheriff, mayor and wealthy wool merchant, Augustine Steward, whose wonky house leans across Tombland Alley, rebuilt much of Elm Hill. The only thatched building to survive in Elm Hill was the Britons Arms and just five other thatched buildings remain in the city.

Britons Arms, Elm Hill

Thirteen priory men were killed. When he heard about this, while attending his parliament at Bury St Edmunds, King Henry III condemned 34 young townsmen to be drawn by horses around the city until dead. Others were hanged, drawn and quartered and their bodies burned, according to the old Anglo-Saxon penalty for arson. The woman who set fire to the gates was burned alive. Though the prior was acknowledged to have instigated the riot he got off lightly: he was committed to the bishop's prison and the priory's manors were seized by the Crown.

A century and a half before the Great Fire of London, much of Norwich was to be devastated by its own Great Fires. First, as the historian Blomefield tells us, in 1505 *"was grete part of the cyte of Norwich brent"*. Two years later, two more fires consumed the city centre, helping to explain why so few timber-framed and thatched medieval buildings survive into the modern period.

Blackfriars' Hall at the top of Elm Hill had been ravaged by an earlier fire (1413) and was rebuilt over a 30-year period (1440-70). The family of Sir Thomas Erpingham – whose kneeling effigy still supervises entry through the cathedral's Erpingham Gate – paid generously towards the restoration of the Blackfriars' buildings

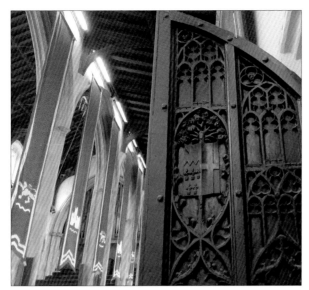

Paston arms on the doors of St Andrew's Hall, hammer-beam roof in the background

while the Paston family paid for the hammer-beam roof in the nave now known as St Andrew's Hall. After the Reformation, Augustine Steward bought St Andrew's Hall on behalf of the city, preserving it as the most complete English friars' church.

In 1509 the city authorities eventually decreed that all new buildings should have roofs of *thaktyle* (tile) and not thakke (thatch). Curiously, this ordinance was repealed in 1532, allowing houses to be roofed in *'slatte, tyle or reeyd'* but sense prevailed and in 1570 thatch of Norfolk reed was again forbidden, changing the appearance of Norwich at the stroke of a pen. In The Netherlands and Flanders, thatch had already been banned in favour of pantiles (after the Dutch 'pan' for tile) that were now being imported all along the east coast of England and Scotland.

Decades after the devastation of 1507, the city still hadn't risen from the ashes. In 1534, to hasten the resurrection, an Act of Parliament declared that if the properties were not rebuilt or at least enclosed within

two years: *'the chief lords of the fees (or 'the mayor &c') may enter upon them, and rebuild or enclose them in one year's time.'* In 1578, in readiness for the visit of Queen Elizabeth, the mayor repaired and beautified the streets although this didn't stop the monarch from commenting on the number of derelict properties.

The city ordinance of 1570, which specified tiled roofs, represented an important turning point for it also outlined steps to fight fires. For instance, every carrier and brewer had to be prepared to convey vessels of water until a fire had been extinguished. For a fire alert, the carriers and brewers were to be called by a peal of bells rung 'auk' or 'auker'. 'Auker' is an elusive word (awkward?) but an inscription on the seventh bell at St Ives, Cambs provides an explanation: *'When backwards rung we tell of fire/Think how the world shall thus expire'*. That is, the call to action was a peal rung backwards. There was also an inspection regime to ensure that church wardens and aldermen maintained sufficient buckets and tall ladders, or else be fined. The thatched St Augustine's church had to maintain six buckets and a ladder, while St Peter Mancroft was a 30-bucketer.

In 1577 the city had its first supply of pumped water, from New Mills, although it took until 1742 for the entire city to have access to water from cisterns. In 1720 a mechanism was installed that raised water into a cistern known as 'The Tombland Waterhouse'. On this site, one hundred and forty years later, JH Gurney was to erect the Tombland obelisk and water fountain, which are still with us today.

In 1668, just two years after the Great Fire of London, Norwich had its first fire engine, kept in St Andrew's Hall; by 1750 the other city parishes had these manual appliances. After the Great Fire, insurance companies sprang up as a hedge against financial loss but it wasn't until 1797 that Thomas Bignold was to set up the 'Norwich Union Society for the Insurance of Houses, Stock and Merchandise from Fire', later the 'Norwich Union Fire Insurance Company'. At that time,

Tombland obelisk and water fountain, erected by JH Gurney (1860) on site of the water cistern

the insurance companies' own trained fire brigades probably offered better fire-fighting than the parish. In 1835 Norwich City Council was allowed to levy a rate to pay for combatting fire, and in 1840 they formed their own fire brigade. This led, in 1858, to the disbanding of Norwich Union's fire brigade whose equipment was passed on to the city. But large companies still maintained their own fire brigades.

In 1876, by the time the City Fire Brigade arrived at a fire in Albion Mills (now apartments) in King Street, JJ Colman's fire brigade were already in attendance. Later that year they were again first attenders when a large fire devastated Boulton & Paul's factory, further upriver at Rose Lane. One of Colman's steam fire-engines can be seen in The Museum of Norwich at The Bridewell but horse-drawn equipment didn't explain their speedy arrival at riverside fires. The black and white photograph shows ten smartly-uniformed firemen of Colman's Carrow Works Fire Brigade standing on a large punt powered by a floating steam engine. By directing eight jets of water into the Wensum they could, apparently, propel the engine along the river.

The Carrow Works Fire Brigade. Image courtesy of Norfolk County Council Library and Information Service.

The Pottergate fire station (1933), accessed through the archway.
©georgeplunkett.co.uk

The city's own fire station had originally been in the medieval Guildhall but in September 1898 a new station was opened in Pottergate. It may have been financially favourable for the council to convert one of their own properties but the downside was that horse-drawn (and later, motor) fire engines had to negotiate their way out through an archway and along narrow medieval lanes. One month before Pottergate fire station was opened, a blaze broke out in the premises of Hurn the rope and sail maker in nearby Dove Street. The municipal fire brigade was assisted by brigades maintained by two of the city's major breweries (Bullards, and Steward & Patteson) but they were unable to prevent the spread of fire to the warehouse of Chamberlin's the drapers, which occupied most of the block. The Norwich Public Library was situated just behind the fire station on Guildhall Hill but it, too, succumbed to the flames. It was eventually replaced in 1962 by a library designed by City Architect David Percival.

In 1935 the fire station moved to Bethel Street, in purpose-built premises designed by Stanley Livock of London Street. Its style, reminiscent of the 'Post-Office Georgian' employed on public buildings of the inter-war years, complements the Scandinavian-influenced City Hall, designed in 1931 but not completed until 1938. Other cities may have had separate fire brigades but not Norwich, for the Chief Constable remained in charge of 'police/firemen' until the late 1940s. This explains the presence of both police and fire helmets carved above the original entrance to the police station in the City Hall.

In 1994, with a horrible symmetry that recalled the 1892 library fire, David Percival's new Central Library (1960-2) burned down, just one hundred yards from the fire station. In 2013 the fire station, behind the City Hall on Bethel Street, became Sir Isaac Newton Sixth Form, leaving the city to be served by three stations, none in the historic centre but on the perimeter at Carrow, Sprowston and North Earlham.

Fire and police helmets above the entrance to police station in City Hall (1938)

Fire at Norwich Central Library 1994. Creative Commons 2.0 Generic Licence. mira66

Norwich coat-of-arms in Norwich City Hall 1938

A city's coat of arms tells us a lot about how the city sees itself and its source of wealth or power. As we will see, there is a more complicated version of the coat of arms but at its most simple the Norwich arms consists of a lion and a castle.

The castle is Norman but the lion may have been adopted about a century later, in the reign of the Plantagenets. In 1194, Richard I granted Norwich the charter in which citizens were allowed to elect their own Reeve – equivalent to the president of the borough. This laid the foundation stone of Norwich's self-government, bequeathing a streak of 'do different' independence that runs through its history. So, it is Richard the Lionheart's lion that appears on the city's coat of arms. In heraldic terms Richard's beast is a *lion passant guardant*. Rather than rearing up on its hind legs, Richard's lion walks across our path, foreleg raised (i.e., passant) while staring at us full face (i.e., *guardant*) , as if to tell us we're being watched.

Henry IV's charter of 1404 granted Norwich county status in its own right, for more than 500 years

flummoxing anyone reading a map that stated, 'The City and the County of Norwich'. This was ended in 1972 when a Local Government Act restructured the ancient counties and Norwich ceased to be one. However, for 568 years Henry's charter gave Norwich, like London, the right to elect its own mayor. To mark this honour, and to administer the new self-governing powers, the city built the Guildhall – the largest medieval civic building outside the capital (1407-1412). Cuningham's map of Norwich (1558) seems to be the earliest surviving map of any English city or town and it advertises Norwich's proud status as '*civitas*' – a form of city state. The same map also shows the Norwich coat of arms as castle and lion on a shield supported by two putti. On another part of the map the royal coat of arms is being held aloft by another two cherubs (*See William Cuningham's map of Norwich on page 21*). Since cherubs flank both coats of arms alike, these creatures could simply be artistic doodling rather than signifying a further upgrade in Norwich's status, yet they continued to appear as supporters of the city arms.

The City of Norwich Arms from Blomefield's History of Norwich 1806

In 1511 the roof of the mayor's chamber in the Guildhall collapsed. The rebuilding of the east wall (1535-7) left us with the distinctive chequerboard of flint and ashlar that probably referred to the building's function as the exchequer where taxes were paid. It also left a further embellished coat of arms: now the angelic supporters were armed with swords and a mysterious object hovered about the whole contraption.

Elsewhere, the mysterious object resolves itself as a hat, perhaps the clearest manifestation of which is on the blue lantern on the south wall of the City Police Station, where it looks like a hat or crown. Former Sheriff Beryl Blower enlightened me further: she said that it was the mayor's ceremonial Cap of Maintenance; the historian Blomefield wrote that the cap was worn by the sword-bearer on all public occasions. If you're interested in these arcane matters I urge you to visit the City Hall (inside and out) to see how many variations of the city's arms you can spot – it really is Coat-of-Arms Central.

The most congested set of symbols I've encountered can be seen on the Norwich coat of arms designed by Thomas Jeckyll and carved by James Minns. This was for the cast-iron 'Norwich' panel that decorated the Norfolk Gates at Sandringham – the stunning exhibition piece of metalwork made by Barnard Bishop and Barnards in Norwich-over-the-Water and given as a wedding present to the Prince of Wales (later, Edward VII). This wooden casting pattern contains the full set of Norwichalia: lion, angels, cap of maintenance and the castle embellished with blind arcading and a mounted knight prancing in the courtyard. However, when I asked the Richmond Herald at the College of Arms about the Norwich arms he upheld the purity of the castle and lion but did not recognise the later additions of cap and flanking angels.

In the post-war period, during the reign of David Percival as City Architect, the city's arms were stripped back to the bare essentials and the motif appears on several public buildings. The reduced arms became decidedly 'modern', the lion tamed, cartoon-like with a hint of Pink Panther.

Bethel Street Police Station 1938. Note the cap above the coat of arms

On municipal housing, Rosary Road 1960

Perhaps the finest examples of lions, the ones that are probably most emblematic of Norwich, are the two bronze statues that guard the City Hall. One of these, in silhouette, also acts as a symbol of Jarrold Department Store. The lions face each other across the steps of the City Hall but in this very act they reveal that they can't be 'Norwich' lions; they may be passant with one leg raised but since they are looking ahead, eyeballing each other, they cannot be *guardant*. This is because they were never designed specifically for Norwich. In 1936, the architects of the City Hall saw Alfred Hardiman's Assyrian-influenced bronze lion at the British Empire Exhibition and commissioned its twin to flank the entrance of the building, completed in 1938.

To the medieval mind dragons were a metaphor for the devil and all his works, the origin of pestilence and plague. This idea of dragons as the embodiment of evil may have evolved from travellers' tales about fabulous beasts or prehistoric fossils or even giant worms; indeed, the Old English for dragon is *wyrm* (or Old High German, *wurm*).

A 'wurm' protecting C13 infirmary doors

A beautiful manifestation of the worm-like dragon can be seen on the thirteenth century infirmary doors from Norwich Cathedral, now in Norwich Castle. The more familiar version, however, is a four-legged, bat-winged creature usually seen writhing at the end of St George's lance.

St George is the city's patron saint after whom two of the city's churches were named: St George Colegate and St George Tombland. Both are beautiful but the latter is the more relevant here for the density of its St George memorabilia. There is a statuette of St George on horseback, a sixteenth century relief of St George, a weathervane font-cover, some Snap the Dragons – much like the ones in the Castle Museum – and a fabulous stained-glass window of St George with a vanquished dragon by CC Powell, 1907. Why do saint and beast feature so strongly in the city's history?

This can be attributed to the Guild of St George, founded in 1385; it became a prominent social institution, celebrating the saint's feast day and performing acts of charity for its members and the needy. In 1417 the power of the guild was greatly enhanced when it was granted a Royal Charter by Henry V, perhaps in recognition of its members who fought alongside him at Agincourt. The charter elevated the status of the guild, making it an influential presence in the city. However, in 1430 the Guild of St George was accused of exerting undue influence on the election of the mayor and it wasn't until 1452 that a peaceful resolution united the guild, with the two bodies sharing officers in the city assembly.

During his continuation of the Protestant Reformation Edward VI sought to abolish bodies that promoted superstition. Perhaps because of its favoured status, the Norwich Guild of St George was allowed to survive by transforming itself into a secular association, the Company of St George. The dragon survived too but now a canvas-covered Snap the Dragon took part in non-religious processions, performing in the annual guild days that coincided with the mayor's inauguration.

This tradition survived, for there are photographs from the latter part of the nineteenth century to illustrate this. These show that a man wearing the dragon suit played a central role in mock pageants held by the Norwich district of Pockthorpe and the nearby village

Snap the Dragon, Norwich Castle

Snap and two Whifflers 1951 ©georgeplunkett.co.uk

of Costessey. In 1951, George Plunkett photographed the Pockthorpe Snap accompanied by two whifflers (from Old English *wifel* for battle-axe) who, historically, twirled weapons to clear the way through the crowd. A nineteenth century engraving also depicts what may be the Pockthorpe Snap in Norwich marketplace one day after the Norwich guild day. The dragon is being taunted by boys who chanted, *'Snap, Snap, steal a boy's cap, give him a penny and he'll give it back.'*

The Pockthorpe Snap – now in Norwich Castle Museum – was bought by Back's Wine and Spirit Shop. For years it hung in their shop entrance in what had been known as Curat's House, an extensive medieval building in Gentleman's Walk now fronted with brick and occupied by FatFace. Many of the shops in nearby White Lion

Back's 'Old Snap'

Street back onto Curat's House and one shop owner showed me paperwork he'd found in the attic. These were invoices on Back's headed paper, depicting the Pockthorpe Snap now tamed and advertising Back's Old Snap Brand Spirits.

Dragon's Hall

There are many other manifestations of the dragon, the best known being the beautifully carved dragon in a spandrel between the roof beams of Dragon Hall in King's Street. In the early fifteenth century this was the trading hall of mayor Robert Toppes who is known to have been a member of the Guild of St George. But where Dragon Hall has a solitary dragon, the refectory in the Great Hospital has three pairs with branched, almost foliate, tails. The dragons in both halls are beautifully carved in a similar style.

A further dragon in the Great Hospital appears in a guise familiar to the medieval faithful who looked to the saints for protection. In St Helen's Church, within the Great Hospital, is a carved pew-end depicting St Margaret of Antioch as she steps out of the belly of the devil in the form of a dragon. Having been swallowed by the dragon, the cross worn by Margaret caused so much irritation that she was ejected, making her the perfect patron for women during pregnancy and childbirth.

St Margaret steps out of the dragon's belly

In 1578 Queen Elizabeth 1 came to Norwich on one of her royal progresses. She is known to have been conveyed from the marketplace to the cathedral; Tudor dragons marked the beginning and the end of that journey. In the Mayor's Court of the Guildhall, adjacent to the marketplace, are two fabulous carvings that declared the city's allegiance to the Tudors. One bench end depicts a greyhound with jewelled collar around its neck, representing the Beaufort line of Henry VII's mother Margaret, while the other shows a writhing Welsh dragon, acknowledging Henry Tudor's Celtic father.

From the Marketplace the queen went to Norwich Cathedral via St John Maddermarket Street where the east wall of the overfull graveyard had to be rebuilt

Tudor dragon on bench end in Norwich Guildhall

Queen Elizabeth I's arms, north wall of cathedral cloisters

St Ethelbert's Gate Norwich Cathedral, restored 1964

in order to widen the street for her procession. On the north wall of the cathedral cloisters, coats of arms were painted of the worthies who entertained her. But pride of place went to the queen's own arms that incorporate the lion of England, which faces the dragon of Wales derived from her grandfather Henry Tudor.

If, that day, the queen had glanced at St Ethelbert's Gate to the cathedral she would have seen a relief carving of a dragon in one spandrel to the right of the arch confronted by an armed man on the other side. We know from a drawing by John Sell Cotman that such a scene was present in the nineteenth century, very likely dating back to the fourteenth century rebuilding of the gate, but what we see today is Frank Beverley's sculpture from the 1964 renovations. The dragon itself can be thought to have a protective role in turning away evil but here it is the armed man (St Michael or St George?) who defends the church from the devil.

The first article I posted on the colonleunthanksnorwich.com blog was on angels' ears. It was based on something that had mesmerised me for many years while I sat at my desk, gazing blankly at a poster advertising an exhibition of the Treasures of Norfolk Churches. The poster featured the fine head of a stained-glass angel, or perhaps a saint. What had intrigued me was that little flap in front of the ear – the tragus – that was split in two, giving it a pie-crust appearance. The double tragus turns out to be a rare genetic abnormality, especially for angels or saints.

Long after the 1980s exhibition at the Sainsbury Centre my wife and I visited St Margaret's church in Stratton Strawless, about 10km north of the city. In this village of poor soil, poor wheat and – so it follows – little straw, we had gone to pay homage to Robert Marsham (1708-1797). Marsham was a local estate-owner and keen naturalist who, by painstakingly recording 27 signs of spring and correlating them with the weather, can be said to have founded the science of phenology. Inside the church was a small exhibition to this pioneer and in a window in the north aisle was that angel's head .

Stratton Strawless angel with double ear tragus

Norwich glass. Burrell Collection, Glasgow

I next saw the double tragus in The Burrell Collection, Glasgow. This was in a fifteenth century stained-glass panel of St John the Evangelist and a kneeling soldier, attributed to The Norwich School. Along with other characters in the panel the saint shared the ear defect; he also shared other similarities with the Strawless angel, including the drawing of the philtrum (the groove between the nose and upper lip) and a distinctive S-shaped curl in the centre of his forehead.

The Burrell glass was said to have come from St Peter Mancroft in Norwich. In 1450-1455 the wealthy wool-merchant Robert Toppes paid for stained glass to be installed in the city's most prestigious church. Toppes (1405-1467) was probably Norwich's richest tradesman at the height of the city's trading power, demonstrating the rise of the merchant class. He became mayor and was member of parliament four times. His trading hall was in King Street, adjacent to the River Wensum that was used to transport his fine cloths and wool for trade with the continent. Then called Splytts, this hall is now

known as Dragon Hall after the carved dragon exposed amongst the roof timbers during restoration.

However, most of St Peter Mancroft's glass was destroyed during the Civil War in what became known as The Great Blow. This was when 90 barrels of gunpowder exploded in the Royalist meeting rooms in nearby Bethel Street. The surviving glass was re-set in the east window and Toppes, two female family members and a third, with a replacement head, can be seen kneeling in a donor panel. Like many other painted figures in this church they display the double tragus.

The question is, to what extent is the double tragus an artistic signature? Expert on Norwich glass, David King – who comes from a line of Norwich glass restorers – detected the styles of three artists in the great east

The Toppes donor panel. St Peter Mancroft

evidently not specific to Norwich glass but, as we will see, there are other features typical of this school.

Norwich had been a regional centre for glass painting since at least the thirteenth century. The Toppes window in St Peter Mancroft is known to have been made in the fifteenth century by the leading workshop of John Wighton. When Toppes was mayor he also paid for alderman Wighton to glaze the council chamber in the Guildhall so it is unsurprising that the figures in the Guildhall glass share family resemblances with those in St Peter Mancroft. Toppes's new rank in life was marked by his own coat of arms, seen between two supporting angels.

In his book on *The Norwich School of Glass-Painters* (1950) Christopher Woodhouse described the dispersal of their work around the county. Several pieces of county glass share superficial similarities with the Strawless head and I decided to make a closer comparison. In previous times I would have done this using tracing paper; instead, I electronically increased the transparency of image files on a computer and, by overlaying each on top of the Strawless head, it was possible to see just how far they correspond. I chose a stained-glass head from St Mary's Warham, one from Bale, and a harp-playing angel at All Saints East Barsham. To a surprising extent, all showed a close correspondence with the Strawless head, confirming an overall facial resemblance that extends beyond double tragus and the S-shaped curl. See opposite.

The exactness with which the Bale, East Barsham, Warham and Stratton Strawless heads coalign suggests the work of a single workshop. More than five hundred years have elapsed, making it difficult to identify individual artists. David King, the eminent authority on Norfolk stained-glass, mentions that John Marsham left money in 1473 to glaze the Stratton Strawless north window. If the Strawless angel was part of the bequest this would date the angel to the 1470s, too late for John Wighton who died in 1458. Wighton's apprentice,

Glass from the Wighton workshop in Norwich Guildhall

window at St Peter Mancroft. And a few years after Glasgow I visited the Metropolitan Museum in New York where I saw a fifteenth century painted-glass panel, again with biblical figures whose ears displayed the double tragus. This time, however, the glass was painted in Gloucestershire. The double tragus is

All Saints East Barsham

William Mundford, left a will in 1457 so he would also have died before the Strawless angel was painted. However, William's son John, who became head of the Wighton workshop, died in 1481 and is therefore a potential candidate. We may never know. What does seem clear is that the cartoon or template on which the Stratton Strawless angel was based originated in Norwich's Wighton workshop and was re-used by its glass painters over several decades.

Stratton Strawless and East Barsham angels' heads overlaid.

Several years after I posted my first article on Angels' Ears I saw an image on Twitter that reminded me of Norfolk's distinctive breed of painted-glass angels.

From All Saints Feering, Essex. Credit: Simon Knott

Simon Knott, who at the time of writing has visited an astonishing 912 Norfolk churches, Tweeted a photograph of a fifteenth century angel from Feering in Essex. I was intrigued by the fact that the feather bonnet worn by this 'Essex' angel seemed very similar to the ones I'd seen on Norfolk glass. Simon told me that the angel from All Saints' Feering was from a mixed collection of Continental and English glass installed by Father Bundock who died in 1989. The 'Essex' angel could well have come from Norfolk. Stylistically, it resembles the Norwich School angels, especially their bonnets.

We saw in the previous chapter that the double ear flap (tragus) is a rare thing yet the 'Essex' angel shares it with angels known to have been painted in Norfolk. Along with other stylistic traits it seems to be diagnostic of glass painted around the mid-fifteenth century in John Wighton's Norwich workshop.

But now it was the similarity between the angels' hats that caught the attention. Sally Badham, former President of the Church Monuments Society, suggested via Twitter, that the headgear could be an *orle*. One definition of an *orle* is a border set in from the edge of a shield, suggesting a heraldic origin. Another that gets us closer to the angel's bonnet is that an orle is the wreath or garland worn around a knight's helmet. *Orle* is also synonymous with torse, an obsolete French word for wreath that, with its implied sense of torsion, suggests it is a twisted thing.

Introduced in the late fourteenth century, the *torse* was a twisted cloth circlet that hid the join between the ornate tournament crest and the knight's helmet on which it sat. The colours in the coil were the same as the wearer's livery colours except, it seems, when the knight wore a lady's favour. Such a makeshift *torse* could be a handkerchief, a ribbon or even the lady's sleeve, twisted into a rope and worn around the helmet.

A torse around the helmet of an angel. Salle, Norfolk

Originally, this twisted coil was something that the knight wore in combat. For comfort, he would have worn a padded, circular *orle* on top of his head to

How to transform a sweater into a chaperon

Portrait of a Man, by Jan van Eyck 1433. National Gallery, London

cushion it from the heavy helm. With the development of lined, padded helmets the *orle* became redundant but it was retained for decorative purposes except now it wound around the outside of the helmet.

Another item – the *chaperon* or *capuchin* – plays a key part in the development of medieval headgear. The chaperon is thought to have evolved from the caped hood, which had a hole for the face with the hood's long tail or liripipe draped down the back. By placing the face-hole on top of the head and wrapping the garment around the head, tied in with its long tail, the hooded cape evolved into a hat that was worn throughout Europe in the Middle Ages. The chaperon appears as a common type of headwear in Early Netherlandish painting whose most famous exponent, Jan van Eyck (d. 1441), wears one in his self-portrait often titled 'Man in a Red Turban'. Although to be technically correct we should call it, *'Man in a Red Chaperon (tied up with its Cornette or Liripipe)'. Capuchin* is still the name for a hood in Dutch.

Examples of men's headwear gleaned from early paintings show how fashions that originated with heraldic dress worked themselves into everyday life. They also transferred to female fashion: a fourteenth century chronicler described how ladies riding to a tournament would affect a masculine appearance by wearing short hoods that were wrapped about their heads by the *liripipe*.

Another suggestion was that the angel's headpiece could be based on the *bourrelet*. Like chaperons, *bourrelets* appear to have originated by rolling up a hood around the head but by the mid-fifteenth century they had developed into a more formal, doughnut-shaped padded roll. In a further development the doughnut-

A simple bourrelet. Lorenzo de Medici, National Gallery of Art, USA

A Principality, from Barton Turf

A Cherubim, Barton Turf

shaped *bourrelet* became transformed into a ring of fabric folded around a framework, possibly made of wire.

To this mix of influences on medieval headgear we can add another garment made from twisted cloth that travellers and crusaders would have seen in the east – the turban.

Clues to the kind of headwear that glass-painters would have seen in mid-to-late fifteenth century Norfolk can be found in this county's outstanding painted rood-screens. The remarkable series of screen paintings in St Michael and All Angels, Barton Turf, illustrates three saints and nine Orders of Angels. In the next figure a Principality from the Third Order of Angels wears – in addition to the crown – what appears to be a twisted *bourrelet* or turban encircling a conical cap.

The winged Cherubim, from the Second Order of the First Sphere of Angels, wears a feather suit and on its head a red, doughnut-shaped wreath with dabs of white, suggestive of feathers.

The full range of pigments available to rood-screen painters was unavailable to glass painters and as a consequence their effects may seem less subtle. Glass was painted with solutions of silver salts, such as silver nitrate, that yielded a narrow range of colours,

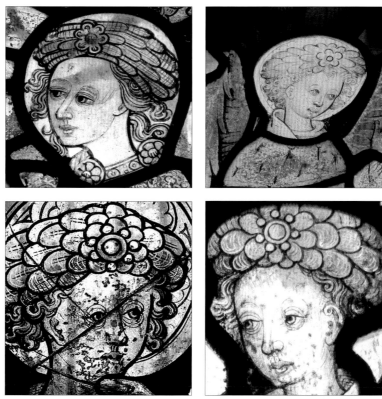

Top left: St Mary's, Burnham Deepdale   Top right: Saints Peter & Paul, East Harling
Left, Feering, Essex ©Simon Knott;   right, Weston Longville, Norfolk © Paul Harley

from pale straw to deep amber, depending on the firing temperature. These colours appear on hair and clothing, leaving the facial features to be drawn in black with three-dimensional modelling provided by subtle shading. It is abundantly clear, however, that painted-glass angels wore feather bonnets studded with a central (possibly jewelled) brooch, of the kind depicted on the Barton Turf rood screen. A fine example is provided by the painted-glass angel from St Mary's, Burnham Deepdale.

An angel wearing a feather bonnet appears in the tracery of the east window at Saints Peter and Paul, East Harling. If made at the same time as the superb main panels then this glass was painted around 1480 by John Wighton's successors in his Norwich workshop. Glass bearing the stylistic hallmarks of this workshop can also be seen in All Saints, Weston Longville where a rather beautiful harp-playing angel wears the twin of the feather bonnet decorated with a seven-pointed brooch that we saw on the angel from Feering in Essex.

As we shall see in the following chapter, angels of that period were depicted wearing feather onesies that ended neatly at neck, cuff and ankles. These were supposedly based on the outfits worn by actors in medieval mystery plays that we know were performed in Norwich. In this case, a feather hat would be the obvious thing to top off an angel's feather suit.

Angels used to be far more common. At one time the faithful would see them painted on church walls and rood screens, depicted in glass, carved in wood and whirring amongst the roof beams. The Reformation and the puritanical iconoclasts changed all that. Some of the angels were targets for potshots although they generally fared better than the images of saints whose faces – closer to earth – were more easily scratched than those of heavenly creatures in the high rafters.

In addition to their feathered wings, these angels tended to be clothed in feather tights, parts of suits that ended neatly at necks, arms and ankles as demonstrated by Archangel Gabriel in St Peter's, Ringland. Such representations appear to have been based on the angel costumes worn by actors in medieval mystery plays. In the beautiful angel roof at St Agnes Cawston, the heavenly beings stand – uniquely – upright at the ends of the jutting hammer beams. They are dressed in suits made of few, but large, 'feathers', suggesting that the players' suits were decorated with flaps of cloth or leather rather than numerous real feathers.

Mystery plays combined with the imagery in churches to project time-worn messages to a largely illiterate audience. But in the thirteenth century, the popularity of clergy who performed in these plays sufficiently upset Pope Innocent the Third that he banned them from appearing. The plays lived on, however, performed by town guilds who dispensed with the Latin and added comic scenes. We know that mystery plays were performed in York and Coventry and one play from Norwich actually survives: this was 'Paradyse', or 'The Fall of Adam and Eve' performed by the Grocer's Guild. The Norwich Stonemasons had their own play, 'Cain and Abel', though the text is lost. Staged on the early summer feast of Corpus Christi, the Norwich guilds are likely to have delivered their parts of the cycle from elaborate 'pageant wagons'.

Archangel Gabriel. C15 Norwich School glass. Ringland

Angel Roof at St Agnes, Cawston

Not all angels were created equal: there were nine orders, ranked according to their importance. Chief were the seraphim who had three pairs of wings: one for shielding their eyes from God, one pair for flying and the third – often represented as a pair of wings crossed over the genitals – for covering their shame. Other orders were the Cherubim (four wings), Thrones, Dominions, Virtues, Powers and Principalities. Archangels, like Gabriel) conveyed messages from God while plain 'angels' mediated between heaven and earth, much like Clarence Odbody (Angel Second Class) who cheered up James Stewart in, 'It's a Wonderful Life'.

Two Norfolk churches contain exceptional late medieval paintings of angels. The rood screen at St Helen's Ranworth (C15) offers a debonair St Michael slaying Satan in the form of a many-headed dragon. Then there is the stunning, painted rood screen at St Michael and

St Michael at St Helen's, Ranworth

Six-winged seraphim. St Peter's, Ketteringham

All Angels, Barton Turf, which largely escaped the depredations of the iconoclasts. These panels offer a rare depiction of The Angel Hierarchy wearing feather suits while some wear headwear fashionable in the late fifteenth century. Archangel Raphael – the leader of the Powers – is depicted wearing his suit of armour while standing on a chained demon whose belly denotes the base appetites that are being subdued here. Only two of the Barton Turf panels were defaced: the face of a Power may have been scratched because it was wearing a papist crown (and no feather suit to mitigate the offence) whilst the Seraphim was caught swinging a censer. Meanwhile, over at the great church of Saints

Archangel Raphael (left) at Barton Turf

SS Peter & Paul, Salle

Peter and Paul, Salle, stone angels (restored) swing censers in the spandrels of the west doorway.

More fragile than wood or stone it is surprising how much painted glass survives from Pre-Reformation Norfolk, much of it from the Norwich School of glass painters. A favourite is the angel at All Saints East Barsham whose feather suit is topped off with a fashionable feather bonnet. In a serene pose the angel plays the harp while, around the county, other Norwich School angels play lutes, bagpipes, citterns and other instruments of the late medieval band. This was one of the angel faces used to demonstrate a family relationships within John Wighton's Norwich workshop. The pose is virtually identical to that of another harpist from Weston Longville. One of the glories of our region is the large number of roof angels, of which more than 80% are found in East Anglia. Why should that be? A possibility offered by angel roof expert, David Rimmer, is based on the Lollards, so named because they were said to mumble at prayer (from Middle Dutch *lollaert*, meaning to mutter). The Lollards followed the heretic John Wycliffe who, over a century before the break with Rome, objected to the pomp, imagery and idolatry of the Catholic Church. Their first martyr, burnt at the stake in London 1401, had been priest at St Margaret's Kings Lynn. A few years later, the first angel roof in East Anglia appeared in St Nicholas King's Lynn so this could be seen as a counterblast to the Lollardism that was rife in the region. Norwich's Lollards were burned in Lollards' Pit, just over Bishop Bridge from the cathedral.

Norwich itself has five angel roofs: St Mary Coslany, St Michael at Plea, St Peter Hungate, St Giles and St Peter Mancroft. St Peter Mancroft has a particularly fine mid-fifteenth century roof where angels cap the ends of hidden hammer beams. Knapton in north-east Norfolk has double hammer-beams that span a prodigious 70 feet, allowing angels to be stacked, double-deckered, at the end of the beams. Together with two rows of angels on the wall plates this forms a heavenly host 138 strong.

Glaswegian artist Charles Rennie Mackintosh came to draw this in the dying years of the nineteenth century. On his tour with friends he also sketched the life-size Cawston angels standing on the jutting beams: Olympic divers waiting for the starting signal.

The age of roof angels dwindled with the Reformation and the puritanism that followed. Few new churches were built for hundreds of years and if you do see angels in Post-Reformation churches they will almost certainly be without their feather costumes.

All Saints, East Barsham

All Saints, Weston Longville ©Paul Harley

Angel Roof at SS Peter & Paul, Knapton ©Paul Harley

The Dukes of Norfolk are conspicuously absent from the county that bears the name of their title. They are now established in Arundel Castle, Sussex, and only traces remain of them in their former county town of Norwich. But before scouring Norwich for vestiges of the Dukes of Norfolk let's look at the ebb and flow of power and religion since this lays the foundation for their later absence.

Thomas Howard 3rd Duke of Norfolk. By Holbein the Younger
© National Portrait Gallery

Earlier lineages of the Dukes of Norfolk had petered out so, in the latest line, John Howard was created the First Duke of Norfolk in 1483 by Richard III as reward for helping him usurp the throne. Then, at the Battle of Bosworth, Howard died along with Richard III when struck in the face by an arrow. Howard's son (the Earl of Surrey) also fought at Bosworth and was placed in the Tower of London by the victor, the Welsh king Henry Tudor (Henry VII), who stripped the earl of lands and title. Henry restored Surrey's junior title but it wasn't until the reign of Henry VIII that the dukedom itself was restored to the next in line, Thomas Howard, Third Duke of Norfolk, who had helped defeat James IV at the Battle of Flodden.

As a religious conservative the Third Duke challenged the reforms brought in by Henry VIII's chief minister, Thomas Cromwell, but Norfolk gained the upper hand when Cromwell fell out of favour for promoting the king's unsuccessful marriage to Anne of Cleves. Hans Holbein was sent to paint Anne's portrait, which Henry claimed was not a true likeness : *She is nothing as fair as she hath been reported.'* It is claimed that Henry found her plain, unsophisticated and poorly educated and the marriage was unconsummated. For all of this Cromwell took the blame and was accused of treason. It was Norfolk who tore the Order of St George from around Cromwell's neck. Norfolk had taken exception to a low-born person having risen so high and was delighted to see Cromwell beheaded as a common man.

But the wheel of fortune never stops, especially not for a man unfortunate enough to have been uncle to both of Henry's beheaded wives. The first of Norfolk's hapless nieces was Anne Boleyn (Wife Two) from Blickling, some 14 miles north of Norwich; the second was Catherine Howard (Wife Five) who Henry married on the day that Cromwell was beheaded, just three weeks after divorcing Anne of Cleves (Wife Four). It was Catherine's supposed promiscuity that led to her execution and the Howards' loss of power. The Third Duke was condemned and placed in the Tower.

The Third Duke's son, Henry Howard (the Poet Earl), has been called: *'the most folish prowde boy that ys in Englande.'* Henry Howard unwisely improved his coat of arms in the family's Kenninghall Palace in South Norfolk by quartering them with the royal arms of his ancestor, Edward the Confessor. Henry VIII regarded competing claims of royal descent as treasonous so Howard, who as a young man had been made to witness the execution of his relative Queen Catherine Howard, was himself beheaded aged 30.

His father, the Third Duke was also waiting to be beheaded in the Tower but was reprieved by Henry VIII's death the day before the planned execution. Henry's daughter, Bloody Mary, had burned Norwich Protestants at Lollards' Pit on the banks of the Wensum and when she became queen she rewarded the staunchly Catholic Howards by restoring their Norfolk dukedom. However, when Henry's other daughter – the staunchly Protestant Elizabeth – became queen the Third Duke of Norfolk was found guilty of plotting against her and so, once more, the wheel turned and lands and title were forfeit to the Crown.

The Fourth Duke of Norfolk, Thomas Howard, is said to have commissioned Thomas Tallis' 40-part motet *Spem*

Henry Howard, Earl of Surrey © National Portrait Gallery

in Alium. After hearing of the 40-part mass that Striggio composed for Cosimo I de' Medici in the 1560s, Howard asked, *'whether none of our Englishmen could sett as good a songe.'* For this alone he is my my favourite Norfolk. During the 2010 Norfolk and Norwich Festival I heard *Spem in Alium* played in St Peter Parmentergate on King Street. Janet Cardiff had arranged 40 speakers so that the audience could walk around and listen to recordings of each of the 40 voices played through its own audio channel. Magical.

After all this time, what remains of the Howards in Norwich? In 1544 the Third Duke's son, (that *most folish prowde* boy) had begun building a sumptuous mansion on the site of St Leonard's Priory given to the Norfolks by Henry VIII, situated high above Bishop Bridge where the Lollards had been executed. From its location overlooking the city, with the cathedral just below, the mansion on St Leonard's Hill was the

Lollard's Pit pub near the site of execution

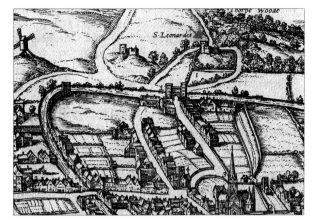

Mount Surrey, arrowed. Braun & Hogenberg's map 1581

Thomas Howard's arms far left, in Surrey House

perfect expression of the earl's hubris. Five years on, after Surrey was beheaded, Robert Kett's army used the mansion as its headquarters where they detained their more important prisoners. From this commanding site, Kett's gunners were able to fire down and damage the fortified superstructure on Bishop Bridge (illustrated on the map), softening the defences so that his followers could enter the city. After the uprising, the site of Mount Surrey was so thoroughly demolished that when local historian Walter Rye bought and excavated the site in 1902 he could only detect traces of the priory gatehouse.

The Poet Earl had also begun building another mansion in the city itself. This was Surrey Court in Surrey Street, which was was barely finished by the time of his execution. Here, between 1901 to 1906, George Skipper was to build Surrey House (also known as The Marble Hall) for Norwich Union, now Aviva. Seventeenth century versions of the Howard's stained-glass coats-of-arms were saved from the old house and installed in Skipper's masterpiece, where they can be seen on the stairs.

Around 1540, on what is now the site of the Duke Street Car Park, the Third Duke (Thomas Cromwell's nemesis and father of the 'folish' boy) built his own palace as a copy of Surrey House on the other side of the city. This

is where the Fourth Duke wooed the devoutly Catholic Mary Queen of Scots with talk of marriage that earned him Elizabeth I's disapproval. In fact, the duke married Mary Fitzalan, the Earl of Arundel's heir, which is how Arundel Castle became the seat of the Dukes of Norfolk. But it was because of the duke's entanglement with a Catholic conspiracy to enthrone Mary Queen of Scots that he was executed by Elizabeth. Once more, Norfolk lands and titles reverted to the Crown. It wasn't until 1660, during the Restoration, that these were restored to the Fourth Duke's great-great-grandson who was held in a mental asylum in Padua; when he died, the title passed to his brother, the Sixth Duke. What tangled webs.

In the early 1670s, the Sixth Duke proposed to reestablish his family's presence in Norwich by rebuilding the Duke's Palace in the modern Italianate style. It was never completed and this seems to have

The Duke's Palace, north side. ©Norfolk County Council at Picture Norfolk

been due to problems with the site. In 1681, Thomas Baskerville didn't hold back when he said: (it is) *'seated in a dung-hole place ... it hath but little room for gardens ... and is pent up on all sides ... with tradesmen's and dyers' houses, who foul the water by their constant washing and cleaning their cloth.'* As we know from the chapter on the Blood Red River, waste was still being emptied into the Wensum from adjacent dyeing houses some 200 years later. The site is marked on Samuel King's eighteenth century map.

Site of the Duke's Palace on King's map (1766)

Photographs from the early twentieth century testify to the devastating effects of flooding on Bullards' Anchor Quay Brewery and on Magdalen Street, both just a few hundred yards away. Built so close to the Wensum, the Duke's Palace would not have been immune from its waters. One reason given for the abandonment of the palace in 1711 was that the cellars had been sunk so deep that the damp compromised the foundations, causing the floors above to subside.

A further reason given for the Eighth Duke's departure from Norwich was the mayor's refusal in 1708 to allow him to process into the city with his comedians and trumpeters. Superficially, this does make the mayor out to have been a killjoy but there are deeper currents. Local historian Blomefield records that in 1683 the Earl of Arundel had brought letters from Charles II (who made a death-bed conversion to Catholicism) limiting the ancient rights of the Norwich Assembly.

Charles' successor, the Catholic James II, also tried to impose direct control upon the Assembly. In 1688 Henry Duke of Norfolk rode into the marketplace at the head of 30 knights and gentlemen and declared for a free parliament; that is, that Catholics should be free of a test that had effectively barred them from both Houses of Parliament. This was the year that the Norwich 'rabble' rioted and burned a popish chapel and houses. Charitably, the mayor's refusal to permit the duke's procession can be seen as a sensible precaution against stirring up the Protestant mob but now that the intensely Anglican Queen Anne was on the throne the Assembly may have felt safe in thumbing its nose at the Catholic nobility after years of interference.

What remains of the palace? It has been mooted that stone columns – a rarity in Norwich – supporting the portico of Mayor John Harvey's house at Number 20 Colegate may have been recycled from the Duke's Palace. Not all of the palace was pulled down, for the

Stone doorway No 20 Colegate

Former chapel of the Duke of Norfolk on St Andrew's Street, 1936
©georgeplunkett.co.uk

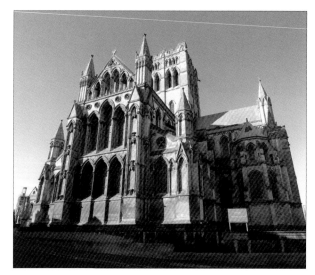

Cathedral of St John the Baptist, Norwich

domestic wing was leased to the Corporation in 1711 as a workhouse, as labelled on King's map. To make this wing more habitable as paupers' dormitories, the Court of Guardians of the Poor inserted a great number of dormer windows into the former bowling alley; the floors below provided workrooms.

Another connection with the Duke's Palace persisted into the twentieth century. In 1764 the Tenth Duke built a Roman Catholic chapel with a chaplain's house on the site, on St Andrew's Street, but in 1794 his successor – who was Anglican – let the chapel to the Norwich

Public Library. This was sold to the Norfolk and Norwich Museum in 1839. Later it became Municipal Offices housing the Guardians of the Poor, later for Public Assistance, but by the 1960s the building's civic usefulness was coming to an end and became home to a billiard hall. This was demolished to make way for the Duke Street Car Park.

A presence in the city was re-established in 1910 when Henry Fitzalan Howard, the 15th Duke of Norfolk, built the Roman Catholic Church of St John. From its vantage point on the site of the old city gaol, high on the west side of Norwich, it now peers down upon the city much as the ancestral Mount Surrey had overlooked the east side some 360 years before. This fine building, which became a cathedral in 1976, is all lancet windows, built in a revived Early English style favoured by the duke.

Old maps show one final, tantalising trace of the seventeenth century Howards – 'My Lord's Garden' – but I'm reserving that for the chapter on Norwich pleasure gardens.

Norwich grew rich from the export of worsted, the fine woollen fabric that took its name from the nearby village of Worstead, but between 1535 and 1561 there was a rapid decline, probably due to the success of lighter foreign fabrics known as the New Draperies. In 1566, in an attempt to revive the city's textile trade, the mayor persuaded the Fourth Duke of Norfolk to ask permission from Queen Elizabeth I to invite *'thirty Douchemen of the Low Countreys of Flaunders'* each with up to 10 family members or servants. The group of 24 'Dutchmen' and six French-speaking Walloons that arrived in Norwich represented a new wave of immigrants – Strangers – whose name lives on around the city.

Thomas Sotherton was the mayor who played a key part in inviting the master weavers to Norwich in expectation that they could manufacture the new fabrics that were becoming difficult to import from the Low Countries. However, the council refused to sanction what they saw as competition and the mayor was forced to admit the foreign weavers under his own seal. There is evidence that at least one family of Strangers rented accommodation in his house, which later became known as Strangers' Hall, now a fine museum of domestic history.

The word 'stranger' is derived from the Old French for foreigner – *étranger*. Although the word is now synonymous in Norwich with the immigrants from the Low Countries (and, a century later, the French Huguenots), 'stranger' had previously applied to anyone who came from outside the city. This was not, of course, the first wave of immigrants: the local historian Francis Blomefield stated that Flemings came to Worstead in the twelfth century; then in the fifteenth century Phillippa, Queen of Edward III, encouraged her 'good and trew weevers', the Flamands (French Flemish), to come to Norwich and Norfolk.

The Sotherton room in Strangers' Hall

In Norwich Cathedral cloisters

Crow-stepped gables. Norwich Cathedral precinct

By 1400, trade between Norwich and the Low Countries was deeply entrenched: 137 'aliens' were recorded as living in the city c1440; in 1426 John Asger from Bruges was Norwich Mayor; and Brice the Dutchman left his mark in the form of the Green Man roof boss in the cloisters of Norwich Cathedral. For carving this foliate head Brice was paid four shillings and eight pence. Another legacy from the Low Countries can be seen in the form of crow-stepped gables (and the round-topped Dutch gables) that occur along the eastern seaboard, from Scotland through East Anglia and down to south-east England.

But in 1567, the year following the arrival of the 30 families, there was a far greater influx, this time of religious refugees. Philip II of Spain was determined to eradicate the Calvinistic brand of Protestantism from that part of the Holy Roman Empire over which he ruled. This was the Spanish Netherlands, comprised of most of modern Belgium and Luxembourg, as well as parts of northern France, southern Netherlands, and western Germany with the capital being Brussels. To enforce the Inquisition the brutal Duke of Alba led 10,000 Spanish soldiers, killing hundreds of Protestants and forcing thousands to flee.

Spanish Netherlands (grey) c1700. Wikipedia

Possibly mindful of religious zealotry, Queen Elizabeth I commanded the Bishop of Norwich in 1568 *'to make a detailed return of the whole body of strangers.'* The census showed that 1,480 of the arrivals were Dutch speakers (the Dutch language being a lower form of the German language, Deutsch) and 339 French-speaking

Walloons. However, the majority of the 'Dutch' came from Flanders while some of the Walloons also came from Flanders as well as what is now northern France. Boundaries have changed but we are talking about an area oscillating around modern Belgium. Indeed, an oration to Queen Elizabeth I on the reverse of Braun and Hogenberg's map of Norwich (1681) refers to 'Belgic friends'.

By 1571 the Norwich Strangers numbered just short of 4,000. There was no corresponding census of native English but it is thought that the immigrants made up about a third of the population. A letter home urged a family member to bring *'two little dishes to make up half a pound of butter ... for here it is all pig fat'*. Another reported, *'You would never guess how friendly the people are together'*. But these were early days.

The mayor succeeding Sotherton, Thomas Whalle (1567-8), was not supportive of the Strangers *'for they did but sucke the lyvinge away from the English'*, but he failed to expel them. A more disturbing event occurred in 1570 when John Throgmorton, gentleman of Norwich, conspired *'to expulse the strangers from the city and the realm.'* Upon *'the sound of a trumpet and beat of drum'*, men recruited at Harleston midsummer fair and at 'Bongey and Beccles' would march upon Norwich where they would fund their enterprise by stealing the mayor's plate. This was only 21 years after Kett's Rebellion and it is jarring to read that a member of Kett's family, Thomas Ket, should have betrayed his co-conspirators, resulting in Throgmorton and two others being hanged, drawn and quartered.

The two languages continued to separate the Dutch speakers and the French speakers. St Andrew's and Blackfriars' Halls had been bought for the city by Augustine Steward after the Reformation, but for over 300 years Blackfriars was known as the Dutch Church. For a while they also worshipped at St Peter Hungate, which had been the Pastons' church when they lived in Elm Hill.

The French-speakers were permitted to worship in Bishop Parkhurst's chapel in the Cathedral. Parkhurst had gone into exile under Bloody Mary's reign and would have been especially sensitive to religious intolerance. In 1637, however, these Walloons moved to the 'hidden' church of St Mary-the-Less, tucked away in Queen Street, Norwich.

St Mary-the-Less

Elizabeth's census of 1568 shows that although the Dutch population was predominantly associated with weaving it contained a self-sufficient community of potters, bakers, school teachers, doctors, gardeners etc. Indeed, it may have been the Dutch interest in horticulture, and their annual Florists' Feasts, that led to this city's preeminence in the world of botany – certainly, the founder of the Linnean Society, Sir James Edward Smith, thought so. This community also had their own pastors of whom the most well-known was English-born Johannes Elison (1581-1639). When he and his wife returned to Amsterdam their wealthy son commissioned Rembrandt to paint their portraits – two of only three full-length portraits that he painted.

The two communities were also divided by the kind of material they wove. A seventeenth century author John Taylor wrote that the various 'stuffs' had *'more hard names than any Apothecary hath upon his Boxes or Gallypots.'* The Dutch were only allowed to make baytrie, 'wet greasy goods' that had been wetted, cleaned and thickened. The Walloons produced 'dry woven goods' known as caungeantry woven from yarn composed of long, combed, parallel fibres that could be woven with lighter yarns such as flax or silk. While the new 'Norwich Stuffs' produced by the Walloons grew in popularity, demand declined for the thicker, plain 'bays' produced by the Dutch. The name lives on in the green baize – from the Old French, *baies* – used to cover billiard tables.

There was strict control over the standard of cloth. In 1571 a *'Book of Orders for the Straungers of the Cittie of Norwiche'* laid down 24 articles for the manufacture of textiles; in addition, 'Sealers' or 'Searchers' were appointed to inspect every piece of fabric in Sealing Halls. Whoever contributed to less than perfect material (dyer, weaver, finisher) was fined and very poor goods were torn in two. Satisfactory goods produced by members of the Norwich Weavers' Company received a lead seal with the city arms (castle and lion) or with NO/ RWI/CH on one side and the surname initials of that year's wardens on the other. The separate identity of Strangers and their products was emphasised by the fact that their seals had neither castle nor lion while their faulty material was sealed with 'aleyne' (alien) in a ring.

The city carefully regulated the Strangers' lives and trade: for example, they could not stay out after the striking of St Peter Mancroft's eight o'clock bell and they could lodge no other Stranger for more than a night without obtaining the mayor's permission. In response to these restrictions the Strangers sent a letter to the Queen's Privy Council numbering the advantages they brought, including: manufacture of textiles not previously made in the city; increased employment; the money they paid the council (and they paid double the national tax or 'subsidy'); they were law-abiding and God-fearing and looked after their own poor. In return, the Privy Council informed Norwich Council that the Strangers had the Queen's endorsement for she wished the citizens *'to continue your favoure unto them'*.

In 1578, Queen Elizabeth I came to see her new subjects for herself. Upon entering St Stephen's Gate she was greeted with a pageant performed by the *'artizans strangers'*. This took place on a long platform

Norwich Weavers' Co. seal. Photo: bagseals.org

on which young girls spun worsted yarn surrounded by loyal mottoes and paintings representing aspects of textile manufacture. The Dutch minister presented the Queen with a *'very curiously and artificially wrought silver-gilt cup'*, worth £50 and in return the Queen gave £30 for the poor Strangers. The queen is said to have watched another pageant from a rear first-floor window of Augustine Steward's house in Elm Hill. Steward's House is now the Strangers Club, founded in 1927 to entertain guests from out-of-town. Just visible to the left is Blackfriars' Hall, at one time the 'Dutch Church'.

Despite the friction between residents and newcomers the Norwich textile trade continued to flourish, the Strangers married into local families and their otherness gradually faded. 'Outlandish' names on the original list of 30 incomers, such as Jerusalem Pottelbergh and Ipolitè Barbè, either died out or were anglicised. Dutch names mutated towards the English: James Minns the Victorian carver was a descendant of Mins; the Muskett family into which Clement William Unthank married were originally Mosquaert; De Witt became White; and Goez and Rumpf became Goose & Rump the Victorian printers.

About a century later, Norwich was to receive a further wave of religious refugees – the Huguenots. While Phillip of Spain was harrying Protestants in the Spanish Netherlands (including French-speaking Walloons) the French monarchy was persecuting its own Protestants. Following the St Bartholomew's Day Massacre (1572) in which 5,000-30,000 Parisians were killed, a degree of religious tolerance was granted by the Edict of Nantes but when this was withdrawn in 1685 many French Protestants fled the country. Some settled in England and some came to Norwich, including the well-known Martineau family. The French Huguenots are associated with the development of 'Norwich crape', a mixture of worsted and silk, but though they have weaving in common with the incomers of the 1500s these later arrivals represent a different historical strand.

Augustine Steward's house, Elm Hill

Headstone, Jan/John Dutchman, St Mary's Hickling

In 1948, Kent and Stephenson published 'Norwich Inheritance'[*1], a book celebrating the city's ancient buildings. That close to the end of war you would have excused them for concentrating on losses due to enemy bombing; instead, with an upward tilt of the chin, they focused on what had been saved, using it as a rallying point for the way this elegant city could look again.

The slum clearances of the first half of the twentieth century had removed much of the insanitary in-fill around the mansions of the long-departed rich but these campaigns can seem over-zealous to us now for they also destroyed much worth preserving. Added to this, the City of Norwich Plan, 1945, looked to a future based around the automobile, new roads, the city's own newfangled 'pedestrian precinct' and a flyover. This car-based future posed its own threat to the texture of medieval Norwich. As the authors said, there was *'a danger of throwing away this heritage … for a commercial conglomeration of humdrum mediocrity.'* How right that turned out to be, with the never-completed Anglia Square development parachuted on top of the Gildencroft/Stump Cross area.

Kent and Stephenson were concerned that little would be left in 50 years' time so they catalogued 20 doors of historic interest. They wrote: *"Fine medieval, Tudor and Georgian doorways once abounded in Norwich, but they are rapidly disappearing."* Although I missed their deadline by 20 years I set out to find the doors they had illustrated.

The first six doors are Tudor, where the head of the door is a gently pointed four-centred arch. The curve around each top corner of the door would have been scribed with a compass set to a small radius while a larger radius was used to take another, shallower, curve up to the central point of a depressed arch. The evolution of Gothic architecture involved the blunting of the point, from the tall, spear-like lancet of Early English to the wide, flattened Tudor arch. In some of these late Tudor

1. The Old Bridewell

doors the point had virtually disappeared. This was to be followed by the Classical door cases of the Georgian period.

1. The Old Bridewell

The present four-plank door to the Old Bridewell in Bridewell Alley is not the one illustrated by Kent and Stephenson but the frame survives. George Plunkett said it was the oldest of its kind in the city, dating it to c.1490. In this early doorway the Tudor arch is still noticeably pointed but becomes flatter throughout this period. The carved spandrels either side of this early Tudor door remain though the Gothic grille above it needs urgent restoration.

2. Number 31 Colegate   3. Bayfield's Court in 1935   4. Shaw's Yard, Colegate   5. 29 Magdalen Street
©georgeplunkett.co.uk

2. Number 31 Colegate

Colegate is the perfect street for door hunting. What was 31 Colegate in 1948 is now number 35. Bacon's House was built in the mid-fifteenth century for the wealthy worsted merchant, Henry Bacon, one-time mayor and sheriff. The several rectangles of newer wood set into the Tudor door replaced the letterboxes and other door furniture described by Kent and Stephenson as 'a disfigurement'. An enjoyable feature is the wicket: the door-within-a-door, which has its own carved spandrels.

3. Bayfield's Court, Stump Cross

Bayfield was the nineteenth century owner of one of Norwich's numerous and insanitary courts or yards, just visible through the archway. The carving in the spandrels gives no clue to the date of what is evidently a Tudor doorway. This doorway did not survive the construction of the inner link road for it lay directly beneath the St Crispin's Road flyover, opened in 1972, that bisected Magdalen Street and destroyed the Stump Cross area.

4. Shaw's Yard, Colegate.

The flint-walled building is no longer the Labour Exchange, as described in the book, but the door with its unpointed Tudor door-head lives on. In the right-hand spandrel is the date, 1570, said to mark the second mayoralty of John Aldrich, 12 years after his first. Aldrich was also sheriff in 1551 and a burgess in Parliament in 1555, 1558 and 1572. Colegate was at the heart of the city's weaving industry in Norwich-over-the-Water and it was evidently where master weavers and people of influence made their homes at a time when Norwich was the nation's second city.

5. 29 Magdalen Street.

Like other such doors that remain in Norwich-Over-The-Water, the one at 29 Magdalen Street was the home of someone made wealthy by wool. The initials in the right-hand spandrel are possibly those of Thomas Shipdham who was at one time mayor then, in 1631, sheriff. The date in the other spandrel is 1612, just beyond the Tudor period but clearly Tudor in style.

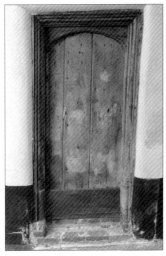

6. Roaches Yard, Elm Hill

7. Garsett House, St Andrew's Street

8. 17 Pottergate

6. In the garden wall of Thorpe Lodge, Thorpe Road (lost)
The door illustrated in 1948 by Kent and Stephenson had been in the wall of Broadland District Council's offices on Thorpe Road. The grocer's arms and a merchant mark in the spandrels revealed this to be the door of George Cocke, Mayor of Norwich in 1613 who lived in Bacon's House on Colegate (see #2 above). The person who brought the door to Thorpe was Colonel John Harvey (1755-1842), one of ten Harvey mayors. The Harveys were probably the most prominent family in the city's textile trade, helping to keep it alive in times of hardship. According to Pevsner and Wilson their properties on Colegate were 'two of the finest early eighteenth century houses in Norwich.' While one branch of the family moved out to the more salubrious surroundings of Catton House, a mile or so north of the city, Colonel Harvey – a leading partner of Harvey and Hudson's Bank – decamped to Thorpe Lodge, a few miles east of the source of his family's wealth. When he moved he took with him a reminder of medieval Colegate.

Having said all this, the door was lost in the 1970s. Instead, I substitute a medieval doorway that would not have been known by Kent and Stephenson for it was only uncovered around 2010 when the render at the side of Roaches Yard off Elm Hill was being repaired. Framing this simple three-plank door is a Tudor four-centred arch with plain spandrels.

7. Garsett House, St Andrew's Street
Garsett (or Armada) House at St Andrew's Plain illustrates, rather incongruously, the transition from Gothic to Classical. This building of 1589 was once much larger until part of it was sliced off to make way for the trams in 1899. The incongruity lies with the Neoclassical Greek Doric porch that has been grafted onto the jettied, timber-framed building. Most porches built in eighteenth century Georgian Norwich tend to be Greek Doric – the simplest classical order, characterised by fluted columns topped with a plain capital. The horizontal frieze supported by the columns is also simple, decorated only by the cricket-wicket-like triglyphs. In the door illustrated in Kent and Stephenson's book the upper two door panels had been glazed to supplement the light admitted by the rather small transom light above. As the eighteenth century progressed this style of light tended to be superseded by the semi-circular fanlight.

9. 46 St Giles under restoration in 2016   10. 48 St Giles   11. Harvey's House 18 Colegate   12. 44 Magdalen Street

8. 17 Pottergate

The Tuscan columns are unfluted and instead of the columns supporting a decorated frieze, as just seen at Garsett House, there is an elaborate keystone. This is a rare example of the use of stone in the city. Kent and Stephenson complained about the 'rash of bells' on the door but the rash has disappeared.

9. 46 St Giles

St Giles is a rather grand street, a terrace of fine town houses once inhabited by the mercantile class. The doorway to number 46 is essentially as it was in 1948: fluted and beaded Tuscan columns supporting a plain portico. Situated above the door is a sun-ray fanlight. Fanlights add height but their presence seems minimised when they are finely cast in metal. Here, the horizontal entablature on top of the columns increases height further – as do the three doorsteps – but, by adding width, the fluted columns restore proportion and grandeur.

10. 48 St Giles

Two doors away is the house built by Reverend Robert Parr in 1792. Above the door is a tear-drop fanlight beneath a decorated Doric frieze. The badly placed YMCA sign of 1948 is no longer present.

11. Harvey's House 18 Colegate

Pevsner and Wilson thought that 18 Colegate was one of the two best early eighteenth century houses in Norwich. 'Harvey's House' was home to wealthy master weaver Thomas Harvey (1710-1772) whose country mansion, Catton House, was a few miles north of the source of his wealth in the weaving district. The appropriately impressive doorway to his town house has fluted Ionic pillars capped by scrolls. Photographer of vanishing Norwich, George Plunkett, remembered a note stating that some of the pillared doorways were based on designs by the city's preeminent Georgian architect, Thomas Ivory. Plunkett suspected that 18 Colegate and 44 Magdalen Street might have been inspired by Ivory. In these examples there is no fanlight although the top panels are glazed.

12. 44 Magdalen Street

This is the other of George Plunkett's two 'best' Norwich doorways. In 1912, the river reportedly rose to fifteen feet above its normal level. The risk of flood explains why some of the Georgian doorways on Colegate and Magdalen Street, as here, were raisedso high above the pavement.

13. Artillery Barracks,
All Saints' Green

14. Gurney Court, Magdalen Street

15. St Catherine's Close,
All Saints' Green

16. 79 King Street

13. Artillery Barracks, All Saints' Green.
In 1771-2, Thomas Ivory – designer of the Assembly House and the Octagon Chapel – built this house for himself. On later maps it appears as Artillery Barracks or Militia Barracks. The door has changed since 1948 but the beauty of the doorway lies largely in the rusticated (cut back) columns and the nine-vaned fanlight. Now it is known as Ivory House.

14. Gurney Court, Magdalen Street.
This was the birthplace of two of the city's eminent citizens: prison-reformer Elizabeth Fry and author Harriet Martineau. Situated in the corner of this small court (now gated) the fanlight above the six-panelled door would have let in welcome light. The hood above it, borne on carved brackets, seems to have been borrowed from the Jacobean period.

15. St Catherine's Close, All Saints' Green.
Around the time that Thomas Ivory built Ivory House (#13 above) he began St Catherine's Close, which

was completed by his son William. In 1948, Kent and Stephenson wrote that the attractive Adam-style porch with its genteel swags was a plaster replica. Possibly, the original was damaged in the bombing raid that destroyed porticos in adjacent Surrey Street (see #19).

16. 79 King Street.
Like Magdalen Street, King Street has suffered much since the war but, fortunately, this Georgian doorway remains as does the Venetian window above. The fanlight based on overlapping Gothic arches differs from the more usual variations on radiating sun rays or teardrops. Contrast this doorway with #9 (46 St Giles) whose height is exaggerated by a fanlight quite separate from the entablature above. Here at 79 King Street the triangular pediment is broken at the base, allowing the fanlight to intrude into the entablature. In the second half of the eighteenth century the broken pediment allowed doorways to be less tall and grandiose (e.g., where dictated by an entrance hall of limited height).

17. 20 Colegate   18. Churchman House, 68 St Giles   19. 25-27 Surrey Street in 1938

©georgeplunkett.co.uk

17. 20 Colegate.

This is the second of the two finest early eighteenth century town houses in Norwich, according to Pevsner and Wilson, the other being #11. Once the town house of Mayor John Harvey, the squat Georgian doorway on this early seventeenth century house is unusual for Norwich in being made of stone. One suggestion is that the stone was recycled from the Duke of Norfolk's Palace on the other side of the river.

18. Churchman House, 68 St Giles (now 71 Bethel Street).

Churchman House, built in the early eighteenth century for Alderman Thomas Churchman, has been described by Pevsner and Wilson as 'possibly the best Georgian provincial townhouse in England'. High praise. The Churchmans were worsted weavers, underlining the point that the wealth of the nation's second city continued to be largely derived from wool. Although the wooden entablature and the triangular pediment are similar to the stone version above (#17), the overall effect here is less squat since the height of the doorway is stretched by inclusion of steps and a fanlight. Inside, the rooms are proportionately tall. I was witness at a wedding here when it was Norfolk Register Office: now you get wed at the Castle.

19. 25 and 27 Surrey Street (demolished).

This terrace is said to have been designed by Thomas Ivory who built houses around the corner on All Saints' Green (#13, #15). The projecting Doric entablature, supported by fluted pilasters and free-standing columns, provided the entrance to two houses, each having a fine door and rising-sun fanlight. The double portico was amongst the finest in Norwich but was destroyed by a fire bomb that landed in the street in 1940. The house has the appearance of a mid-eighteenth century building but George Plunkett noted that when it was pulled down in 1963 various pencilled dates were revealed on the woodwork, including 1692 and 1740. Another inscription read: *'James Rump carpenter and joiner ... Norwich made this portico in the year 1821.'* It is possible that older pieces of wood were incorporated into the structure.

20. 31 and 33 St Giles

20. 31 and 33 St Giles.

These houses were originally built in the late sixteenth/ early seventeenth century and refaced in the late eighteenth century. The houses were not, therefore, built with Palladian proportions in mind so the late Georgian doorway would have been retrofitted to a less generous floor-plan. Spanning two doors with a common fanlight above the entablature required structural ingenuity since a semi-circular fanlight of that width would have been too tall for the narrow, low hallways it was intended to illuminate. Instead, height was reduced by: dispensing with a triangular pediment; ensuring the columns did not extend above the head of the door; and using a narrow segment from a very large circle as a template for the fanlight (and confusing the 'radial' spokes of the fanlight in the process). Contrast this with the tall doorcases given the full Georgian treatment further along St Giles' Street (#9 and #10 above).

The fact that 17 out of the 20 doorways selected by Kent and Stephenson can still be seen today might seem to be cause for optimism. Except that the selection was made of doors still standing after the war. George Plunkett's much larger survey[2] from 1945 includes doorways known to be present before the war but are now absent. This shows how many fine buildings and doorways suffered, not just from the war, but from twentieth century modernisation.

1. Arnold Kent and Andrew Stephenson (1948). Norwich Inheritance. Pub: Jarrold and Sons Ltd, Norwich.

2. George Plunkett (1945). Old Norwich doorways. Norfolk Archaeology vol 28, pp 39-70.

Postscript

Entrances designed to project prestige were not, of course, confined to the three hundred years encompassed by Kent and Stephenson's collection. In a follow-up blog post I made my own collection of 20 doorways; most were Georgian, some were later. The earliest was John Page's hall house built c1330 in King Street. One hundred years later it was owned by the wool merchant Robert Toppes, one of the richest men in the city. He remodelled the entire first floor as his trading hall, which is where the carved dragon was rediscovered in a roof spandrel during the twentieth century. In Toppes's time the building was known as Splytts, now it is Dragon Hall. As part of his renovation,

Toppes altered the original fourteenth century doorway situated in a side entrance off King Street. The low opening under the ogee head was not enlarged but incorporated in a wide, expensive stone surround with a pointed arch containing carved shields in the spandrels.

Toppes was an important man of affairs in the city. To ensure his spiritual wellbeing, and perhaps to celebrate his status as mayor and member of parliament, Toppes sponsored stained glass. Some of this is gathered in the 'Toppes Window' in the east end of St Peter Mancroft where his family is depicted in a donor panel.

Before the railways arrived in the mid-nineteenth century, towns were built from the materials around or beneath them. Aberdeen arose from granite, houses in the Cotswolds – roofs and all – were made of the honey-coloured bedrock on which they stood, but Norwich is so far from decent building stone that only the conquering Normans, rich grandees or the church could afford to import it. So between the age of medieval timber-framed building and the arrival of steel-reinforced concrete Norwich was largely made of wood and of clay in the form of brick and tile.

Around 1860, Norfolk contained 114 brickyards spread throughout the county so although Norfolk may have lacked stone there was evidently no shortage of brick clay. Due to the difficulty of transporting heavy loads, bricks tended to be made close to the building site. The railway came to Norwich in the 1840s, allowing bricks and materials like Welsh slate to be transported more easily and this, combined with the repeal of the tax on bricks in 1850, contributed to the explosion of terraced-house building in Norwich. Surrounding Norwich were the brickyards of Banham, Lakenham, Reedham,

Rockland St Mary, Surlingham and Welborne but the one that perhaps had the greatest effect on the appearance of Norwich – via its red or white decorative products – was the Costessey Brickyard five miles to the west, run by the Gunton family.

Many years ago I saw comedian Ken Dodd at the Theatre Royal Norwich. Part of his introductory schtick was to play with local names, pronouncing Happisburgh as Happy's berg instead of Hay's bruh and Costessey as three-syllabled Coss-tess-ee instead of Cossey. Anticipating his difficulties the Gunton family, who managed the Costessey Brickyard from the 1830s to 1915, called their range of ornamental bricks 'Cosseyware'. In 1882 it employed 40 men and boys.

The origin of the Costessey Brickyard can be traced back to the building of Costessey Hall. When the baronetcy was restored to Sir George Willliam Jerningham in 1824, his 'commanding and forceful' wife became dissatisfied with their old Tudor Hall and wanted a new one. John Chessell Buckler – who had just come second in the competition to design the new Houses of Parliament,

Norwich roofscape from the St Giles car park

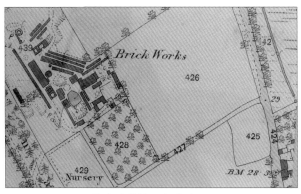

Gunton's Brickworks, Costessey. © Ordnance Survey 1882

destroyed by fire in 1834 – was commissioned by The Jerninghams to design them 'the richest Gothic building in England'. The thousands of bricks used in the construction of this Tudor Revival extravaganza were made nearby in their tenant's brickyard.

The folly was never completed, largely because of the enormous cost, partly through problems of succession. Sir Henry Valentine Stafford Jerningham had no children and in 1862 asked the Masters of Lunacy to declare his heir, The Right Honourable Augustus Frederick FitzHerbert Stafford Jerningham, to be of unsound mind. The last Baron Stafford to live at the hall, Sir FitzOsbert

Costessey Hall in ruins, 1933. ©georgeplunkett.co.uk

Edward Stafford Jerningham, was also 'eccentric' and after he died the building was seen as a white elephant; this led to its long drawn-out demolition, which began in 1920.

The fortunes of the brickworks mirrored the rise and fall of neo-Gothic Costessey Hall. After the Hall, George Gunton began to look for alternative outlets for his decorative bricks. His expansion into the domestic and commercial arena was promoted by the repeal of the brick tax that had been particularly punitive for oversize decorative bricks. Cosseyware began to increase in popularity, first under George Gunton then from 1868 under his sons William and George. It was therefore during the second half of the nineteenth century that Cossey bricks started to have an impact upon the appearance of the nearby city.

The yard's ordinary bricks, known as 'builders', could be made from red or white clay and when Clement William Unthank inherited his father's land around 'Unthank's Road' in the parish of Heigham, he specified that the terraces should be built of Cossey Whites. The quiet uniformity of the early terraces on the south side of Unthank Road can be attributed to this and other restrictive covenants drawn up by the solicitor Unthank.

Trinity Street. Built on the Unthanks' Heigham Estate, Norwich

The Costessey Brickyard also produced 'fancy bricks'. This started with the moulded bricks required for building the elaborate neo-Tudor chimneys that were such a feature of Costessey Hall's complex roofline. These bricks were made in specially carved moulds, often in

Cosseyware chimney bricks in Chapelfield North

decorative details, like the ornate Corinthian capitals, were made of white Cosseyware – a combination he repeated in his Castle Chambers (1877) in Opie Street. Twenty years later, around the corner on Agricultural Hall Plain, he employed red brick for the new Royal Hotel to replace the building demolished to make way for the Royal Arcade off the marketplace. The lower floors of the Royal Hotel are quite plain but look up and you will see that Boardman embellished the upper storeys of this 'free Flemish' building with ornamented string courses, gables and pinnacles, all of which were pressed from carved wooden moulds at the Costessey Brickyard.

small batches. Guntons employed highly skilled carvers who, as well as directly carving unique terracotta panels, are likely to have carved the wooden moulds for batches of fancy bricks.

The influence of the Arts and Crafts Movement, with its emphasis on the English Vernacular Revival, trickled down to middle class houses. And as well as supplying their Tudor Revival chimneys, Guntons made letter and number bricks for spelling out names and white terracotta tracery to mimic Tudor windows. A pleasurable way of seeing Gunton products is to visit the Plantation Garden in Earlham Road. Cabinet maker Henry Trevor made this garden from an old lime and flint quarry; he was a friend of George Gunton and used Cosseyware seconds to make his jumbled walls. About half of the patterns that Guntons used on chimney bricks can be found there.

Cossey bricks are readily spotted throughout the city. Edward Boardman, architect of Victorian Norwich, used red and white clay products to embellish his buildings. His Congregational Chapel (1869) in Princes Street has a classical facade made largely of white bricks but its

Princes Street Congregational (now United Reformed) Church

Gunton's fancy bricks on the Royal Hotel, Norwich

Boardman's offices, Old Bank of England Court, Queen St.

James Minns, known as 'Norfolk's Grinling Gibbons' was a carver of wood who was sufficiently ambitious and skilled to have had a panel accepted by the Royal Academy's Summer Exhibition. Having seen James Minns' photograph I feel convinced that he is the senior craftsman, with trimmed beard and flat cap, who presents the carved shield to a top-hatted Skipper on the Jarrolds' tableau. The panels were installed around 1904. This was the year that James Minns died of heart failure. Senile decay was also listed on the death certificate so perhaps it was his son or other Costessey workers who actually carved this shy craftsman.

Individual pieces of directly carved terracotta are less common. Two fine examples can be seen on the offices of the two pre-eminent architects of nineteenth century Norwich, Edward Boardman and George Skipper. Edward Boardman's offices in Old Bank of England Court off Queen Street are identified by a terracotta nameplate. Larger terracotta tableaux are to be found on the bay windows of George Skipper's offices, now incorporated into Jarrold's Department Store on London Street. After posting the article on Fancy Bricks online, I was elated to be shown a group photograph of Guntons' employees. Peter Mann, whose father and grandfather had been employed at the yard, then named each employee including the 'carvers', James Minns and his son Edward.

The carver shows the shield to Skipper on the Jarrolds tableau

Gothick brickwork had been a major architectural ingredient of the Arts and Crafts Movement but by the turn of the twentieth century the public's fascination was waning and in 1915 the Gunton family failed to renew their lease at Costessey. The family continued making ordinary bricks ('builders') at their Barney, Little Plumstead and Runton works but these outposts closed in 1939 due to fears that the kilns could act as beacons to enemy planes. The last remnant of the Hall is the Belfry Block that still stands, near the eighteenth fairway at Costessey Park Golf Club. But what remains of the brickyard itself? A derelict kiln is reported to stand on private land near the end of Brickfield Loke but if you pass through the West End of Old Costessey you can't miss the fancy bricks on the cottages, some of which George Gunton built himself.

Employees of Guntons' Brickyard pre-1904. © Ernest Gage Collection. Red arrow, James Minns; Yellow arrow, Edward Minns.

The word palimpsest usually conjures a manuscript written on fine animal skin, with the original writing scraped away for the vellum to be used again. Sometimes the previous script grins through and it's in this sense that the word is used in architecture: the ghostly traces that reveal a building's previous lives.

Archway into Orford Yard (2016)

Above the archway into Orford Yard off Red Lion Street, in a building that Edward Boardman designed for John Pollock's veterinary surgery (1902), metal lettering spells out 'shoeing','forge', 'livery' and 'stable'. These words were once commonplace but now they seem archaic. Vehicles propelled by internal combustion engines had been invented some 25 years earlier but who, at the beginning of the twentieth century, could imagine the extent to which horses were to be replaced by cars that would necessitate great changes to the medieval street plan?

The Norwich economy had been sustained for hundreds of years by the weaving industry but, when northern mills began to import cotton, their lighter printed materials presented a severe challenge to Norwich's traditional woollen worsteds. Our geology also worked against us, for northern mills had fast-running water and supplies of coal to run the large power looms. The flatlands of East Anglia, sitting on chalk, were at an obvious disadvantage. And for a variety of reasons, the Norwich weavers were late to collectivise, to move from family units into larger factories. There is little now to remind us that the woollen industry ever existed except, perhaps, for the roof lights – the lucams – that lit the family's hand-loom in the attic (and which can still be seen around the city).

One building that did survive is the Norwich Yarn Company's Mill, built in 1838 as an initiative by the mayor, Samuel Bignold (son of the founder of Norwich Union), to arrest the decline of Norwich's textile trade. Known as St James' Mill it was built on the site of a thirteenth century Carmelite monastery. In a snippy essay about Norwich, in which he found little to praise, the architectural critic Ian Nairn admitted the building to be 'the noblest of all English Industrial Revolution Mills' and helped to gain it listed status. On the third floor, Willett and Nephew had 50 power looms but these were too little too late to stem the tidal wave of fabric

St James' Mill

All that remains of the Co-op shoe factory

Haldinstein's building at 2-4 Queen Street, now known as Seebohm House, was built in 1872 (if we can trust the date on the rain hopper). Its large runs – almost strips – of windows anticipate the steel-framed modernist factories of early twentieth century Germany. This forward-looking building was designed by local architect Edward Boardman, whose offices were 50 metres away in the Old Bank of England Court. However, the pointed Gothic arch at the entrance undermines this bid for modernity; it nods to the Victorian Gothic revival while the door grille is pure 1930s Art Deco. The reason for this architectural mish-mash can be found in the Norfolk Record Office where the original plans confirm that the entrance was designed with the same shallow arch to be found above the windows on the lower floors. But other plans dated June 1946 show, that after George Haldinstein sold his shares to Bally, the ground floor was remodelled and the entrance updated by Boardman and Son (which was then headed by the grandson of the original architect). The building now provides offices for several companies.

emerging from the north. Even the famous Norwich shawls, which briefly gave our weaving industry a flicker of life, suffered the indignity of their teardrop pattern being called 'paisley' after the Scottish town that outproduced us. At one time St James' Mill was used by chocolate manufacturers, Caley's, and by Jarrold's printing Works until a few years ago. Now it houses private offices.

As weaving declined the shoe industry became the major employer and reminders of that trade survive. In the middle of the twentieth century there were about thirty boot and shoe manufacturers employing over 10,000 workers but that trade has virtually disappeared. The Norwich Co-operative Industrial Society's shoe factory in Mountergate was once a major employer but it was replaced by a housing development, Mountergate Court, and only a wall from the old factory remains as a baffle against noise.

Well into the twentieth century Haldinstein's shoe factory occupied seven blocks of buildings between Queen Street and Princes Street in the centre of the city. In the 1930s Haldinstein's went into partnership with Swiss firm Bally but after World War II George Haldinstein sold them his 51% share; by the time production ceased in 1999, Bally was the last shoe factory in the city.

Former offices of Haldinstein's shoe factory

Once the largest shoe factory in the country

A much larger factory – indeed, the largest shoe factory in Britain – was extended by Boardman and Son in various phases from 1876 to 1909. Howlett and White's premises occupied a large block on the corner of St George's Street and Colegate, providing employment for hundreds who, in previous generations, could well have been working in the woollen trade. By the 1980s the once-thriving Norvic Shoe Company was in receivership. Most of the former factory has been converted to private apartments, with some offices, but on the ground floor there is a sixth form academy and The Last Wine Bar – a restaurant that alludes to the cobbler's last and the building's previous incarnation as a shoe factory.

In 1913 another building by Boardman and Son, which is almost domestic in scale, was constructed on Duke Street for the Norwich Electric Light Company. About 20 years earlier the company had converted the old Duke's Palace Ironworks to an electricity generation station, fired by coal boilers. When Boardman and Son were designing these offices the NELC illuminated 1750 lamps around the city, but by 1926 the Duke Street site could no longer cope and the city was supplied instead by the power station at Thorpe. The Duke Street site was converted to offices, a function they retain nearly a century later.

Down Duke Street and over the bridge is a former Board School that provides further testimony to the way in which cities evolve in unpredictable ways, in this case as a result of the democratisation of education. As a result of the 1944 Education Act, secondary education became more open to working class students, especially girls. A generation later there was a corresponding rise in new university building while the last twenty years has witnessed an even greater social shift: that is, the dramatic upsurge in the number of students in tertiary education – certainly, way beyond the imagination of lower income families of the late nineteenth/early twentieth centuries whose children would probably have entered the Norwich trades.

Norwich Electric Light Company, former offices

On the north wall of the red-brick school are two terracotta panels: one represents the Norwich coat of arms; the other, in carved letters, states 'Norwich School Board AD 1888'. Funded by local rates, board schools were built in response to an 1870 Education Act decreeing that towns should establish schools in which the teaching of religion was strictly regulated. Importantly, these were amongst the first public institutions to be open to both sexes. The school was built by J Youngs and Sons (now part of the RG Carter Group) and, like other schools around the country, they built in a style first adopted by London's influential board schools – the fashionable Queen Anne Revival

Former Board School, now part of NUA

century the School of Art and Design expanded into a factory-like building on the opposite side of St George's Street, constructed in 1914 as premises for builders' and plumbers' merchants, Guntons. Later, Frederick Gunton was joined by a forebear of actor Nigel Havers, forming Gunton & Havers.

NUA has also resuscitated a building dear to Edward Boardman. While George Skipper was acknowledged by John Betjeman to have provided Norwich's 'fireworks', the prolific but less exuberant architect, Boardman, quietly got on with the business of transforming an essentially Late Medieval and Georgian city with his forward-looking industrial buildings. He also added the Church Rooms to the Congregational Chapel in Princes Street that he had designed in 1879 – and where he preached. Now known as Boardman House, Church Rooms were refurbished by NUA in 2015 for use by their School of Architecture. The interior has been treated with respect, with laser-cut panels on the central stairs echoing the Victorian ironwork.

with its tall casement windows and high Flemish gables. In the mid 1990s the old school was purchased then refurbished as part of the remarkable expansion of the Norwich University of the Arts (NUA).

Throughout the twentieth century the Norwich School of Art and Design had been confined to the old Norwich Technical Institute (1899-1901) by St George's Bridge. This was established as a junior technical college for the 'industrial classes' but it was soon joined by the old School of Art, which had been unsatisfactorily accommodated in the top floor of the Free Library (now demolished) at the junction of Duke Street and St Andrew's Street. In the latter part of the twentieth

The Gunton building in St George's Street

Inside Boardman House

NUA's East Gallery

Counterbalancing the high moral purpose of Victorian Norwich was the skating rink where fun could be had by gaslight. Built in Bethel Street as a roller-skating rink in 1876 it was then used from 1882 to 1892 by the Salvation Army as their Citadel. This was entered from St Giles Street via the iron gates adjacent to the Army's present building that was once Mortimer's Hotel. I remember the skating rink towards the end of its 100 year occupancy by Lacey and Lincoln, builders' merchants, before it was refurbished by the present owners in the 1980s. Now, Country and Eastern is a spectacular eastern bazaar that also contains a collection of South Asian arts and crafts.

By one of those pleasing circularities, NUA's 'East Gallery' occupies a site where the nineteenth century Norwich School artists once exhibited. This building at the corner of Bridewell Alley and St Andrew's Street formerly housed The Royal Bazaar. An early engraving shows its Great Hall to be a large, high, open space, supported by cast-iron pillars, inhabited by top-hatted men and crinolined women absorbed by demonstrations of science and engineering. The Norwich Society of Artists – Crome and Cotman's brotherhood – had disbanded in 1833 but six years later the artist Thomas Lound became co-founding President of the Norwich Art Union and it was in the Bazaar that the Art Union held its first exhibition. By 1846, Lound was also involved in the Norwich School of Design, a predecessor of the Norwich Technical Institute (1899).

The Old Skating Rink, Bethel Street

Buildings designed by George Skipper tend to be showier than Boardman's. His Surrey House for the Norwich Union was perhaps his masterpiece, with its spectacular marble hall made from stone redirected from Westminster Cathedral after that project had run into financial difficulties. The Poet Laureate and activist for the protection of ancient buildings, John Betjeman, loved it. A small part of its success lies in the fact that it was set back from the street so that it can be appreciated as a spectacle. In the same period (1903-4) Skipper designed another grand Baroque showpiece for those in need of insurance: this was St Giles House for the Norwich and London Accident Insurance Association. Pevsner and Wilson called it 'the Norwich Union in miniature' but it is less approachable than Surrey House; it intrudes upon the pavement in St Giles' Street, giving passers-by little opportunity to appreciate the building face-on. For a while, it became a telephone exchange and was known as Telephone House. In the 1930s, St Giles House became municipal offices housing the Treasurer and Education Departments. It is currently a luxury hotel.

Time travellers from the nineteenth century would be struck by a lack of signs to show that Norwich was once the centre of an agriculturally prosperous county. In their time you would have been pressed into doorways by animals being driven to market. On Samuel King's New Plan of Norwich (1766) there are names such as Hog Hill, Swine Market and Old Horse Fair but these references do not appear on modern maps and only Hay Hill and Cattlemarket Street are left to remind us of the city's former preeminence as a trading centre.

The arrival of the railways in the mid-nineteenth century brought animals from beyond a day's drive and Prince of Wales Road was constructed to accommodate the influx, linking Thorpe Station to the various livestock markets on the streets surrounding the Castle. In 1882 the animals would have been driven past the newly-built Agricultural Hall, which provided a trading floor for all varieties of agriculture. For once, it seems, this was a major project not designed by Skipper or Boardman. Instead, JB Pearce produced a building faced with alien red sandstone from Cumberland, no doubt transported by rail and carted up Prince of Wales Road. The deep red stone is relieved, however, with carvings in red terracotta from Gunton's Brickyard in nearby Costessey. These appear as keystones above the ground floor windows. Some are unidentified heads of dignitaries. The bull's head most probably refers to JJ Colman (Vice-Chairman of the Agricultural Hall Company) whose tins of mustard powder were decorated with this motif. The Prince of Wales feathers allude to both the name of the street and the prince who inaugurated the hall – the future Edward VII, patron of

St Giles House, St Giles' Street

Agricultural Hall

At the back of the old Agricultural Hall, on the east side of Cattlemarket Street, is a building that would have struck an unsettlingly modern note with the mid-nineteenth century farmers who crammed the thoroughfare on market day. Now known as Crystal House it was built in 1863 for Holmes and Sons who manufactured agricultural machines, such as traction engines that would revolutionise the use of labour in the countryside. They also made the 'Norvic' bicycle. Constructed a dozen years after the Great Exhibition this striking building was inspired by Joseph Paxton's revolutionary Crystal Palace. Paxton's genius was to exploit the mass production of large, strong sheets of plate glass to form huge glazed walls supported by thin cast-iron glazing bars – a principle that allowed Holmes and Sons to present their wide range of farm machinery from behind the largest shop window in the city. From 1906 to1983, Panks the engineers were logical successors but succession took a lateral arabesque when the Crystal House was occupied by Langley's toyshop. They were followed by Waring's furniture store and most recently by Bullards' gin distillery.

the Norfolk and Norwich Fat Cattle Show Association. Two years later, Oscar Wilde came to the hall to give a lecture on 'The House Beautiful'. There is no record of what the Fat Cattle men made of this. Today, the former Agricultural Hall is better known as Anglia House, the home of Anglia TV.

The Crystal House, Cattlemarket Street (2016)

Born in Bedford 1930, dead of cirrhosis of the liver 1983, Ian Nairn wrote about towns, not as a trained architect but as an outsider. In 1955 he produced a maverick edition of Architectural Review entitled Outrage in which he railed against the homogenising effect of bland postwar development and the blurring of lines between town and country. He introduced the word 'subtopia' for the nondescript urban sprawl that threatened to consume the entire country: *'the end of Southampton will look like the beginning of Carlisle.'* He also wrote about Norwich ... and not in a good way.

The entrance to the city, from a bus

In the early 1950s, Nairn was stationed on the outskirts of Norwich at RAF Horsham St Faith, now Norwich Airport. In 1967 he produced an architectural review of 'Britain's Changing Towns' and it was probably to the city's detriment that Norwich was the only one in which he had actually lived (other than London). The two uneventful years he spent on the celestial Unthank Road with his first wife, Joan Parsons, allowed him far longer to polish his hostility than was possible for his other provincial visits. In a recent book, Gillian Darley and David Mackie thought Nairn's essay on Norwich to be *"particularly rancid"*.

Nairn said, *'... the traveller comes on a brand-new building announcing the city centre at the southern end of St Stephens Street, which for crushing banality must have few equals in Britain ... to come first in a field as large as this is no joke.'* In this at least, Nairn was right. After St Stephens Street was flattened in the war it was decided there was nothing worth saving except – according to Pevsner and Wilson – AF Scott's 1912 Adam Revival building for Buntings Department Store, now Marks & Spencer. Taking the opportunity to widen the road, the entire south-east side was demolished. In a lacklustre tribute to the lost towers of St Stephen's Gate – through which Queen Elizabeth I had entered the city - the major port of entry from the south was defined by two curved buildings, one of them the St Stephen's multi-storey carpark. In a postscript, Nairn wrote that the rebuilding of St Stephens Street was, *'probably the worst thing of its kind I have ever seen in what passes for a cultured city.'*

On the other hand, he loved George Skipper's 'old' Norwich Union building (1900-1912) in nearby Surrey Street, calling it, *'a super-Palladian palace which is as good as anything of its style in the country.'* But the adjacent modern headquarters (1960-1), designed by TP Bennet and Sons, he thought a completely anonymous slab. Like his fellow architectural commentator, John Betjeman, Ian Nairn approved of our local architect,

Surrey House, designed by Skipper

125-129 King Street in 1936 © georgeplunkett.co.uk

MAGDALEN STREET, NORWICH 1958-59

© Civic Trust

identifying the Telephone Manager's Office in St Giles Street as, *'another firework by Skipper ... smaller but if anything even richer.'*

Nairn loved the unlovable; he was neutral about historic Elm Hill, *'with its cobbles and antique shops'* but he outrightly condemned the decline of Pottergate and King Street. Despite suffering from faceless post-war infill, Pottergate manages to thrive as part of a vibrant mix of independent shops in the rebranded 'Norwich Lanes'.

King Street, however, has changed more dramatically since Nairn's visit. A photograph taken by George Plunkett shows 125-129 King Street as it was in 1936 but in the 1960s or 70s the ground floor of this building was ripped out and the shop fronts replaced by concrete piers and plate glass. The full horror can be seen now that the shop is derelict. This medieval building is adjacent to Dragon Hall, one of the 'Norwich 12' iconic buildings. Once known as Splytts, this wool-trading hall backs onto the St Anne's Wharf housing development being built on the site of a Victorian foundry and part of the old brewery. Modern town houses on the opposite side of King Street were built in a uniformly modern 'heritage' style and so the accretion of character,

developed over centuries and still visible in Plunkett's photographs, has all but evaporated.

Nairn said that the spirit of the Coslany ward in Norwich-over-the-Water had been stifled by *'over-zoning and carelessness'*. In the first of their redecoration schemes (1959), the Civic Trust attempted to revive Magdalen Street. Facades were stripped of unnecessary clutter and painted in pastel shades from a palette of 18 colours and 13 alphabets selected by Coordinating Architect, Misha Black. The Times reporter gently mentioned the resulting 'Walt Disney effect' while Nairn wrote that the pastels were, *'cruelly out of touch with the local colour-range, and after five years it looks as jaded as last year's fashion.'*

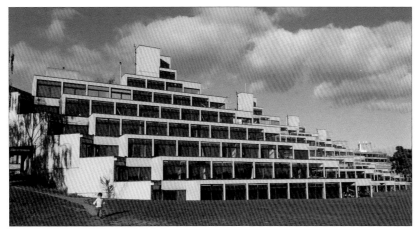

Lasdun's ziggurats at the University of East Anglia

One of Nairn's bright spots was Denys Lasdun's University of East Anglia. Lasdun designed the campus to face the newly-excavated lake with the 'teaching wall' behind; this was separated from the ziggurats (the stepped boxes providing student accommodation) by an elevated walkway. In his 1967 postscript, Nairn was evidently minded to approve this icon of New Brutalism sight-unseen since building had barely begun. Who knows what he would have made of the subsequent additions to the University Plain.

Nairn did concede that there were still many marvellous things to see in Norwich, including, *'one of the great town views of England.'* This would be from the escarpment to the east, from which the cathedral can be seen to dominate the city. Despite setting himself up by saying that the cathedral had never received the praise it was due, his own tribute was muted: *'no fireworks'*. Nairn did like the Perpendicular vaulting added to the Norman nave by Bishop Walter Lyhart after fire destroyed the timber roof in 1463; he thought it *'a splendid match for the three-storey elevation underneath.'* Designed by Reginald Ely just after he completed King's College Chapel in Cambridge, it is a glorious stone roof, a masterpiece of late medieval craftsmanship, but you would hardly

call the cathedral's new roof a 'match' since it is hard to disguise the stylistic chasm between the delicate lacework of lierne ribs and the ponderous Norman piers made of lighter Caen stone that had been turned a pinkish hue by the fire.

Lierne roof, Norwich Cathedral

St George Colegate

Of St Peter Mancroft, Nairn said nothing about one of the best angel roofs in the country, nor of the outstanding fifteenth century Norwich School glass in the great east window. Instead, he thought the building, 'one of the most neurotic and inconsistent designs that ever received universal adulation.' Nairn's complaint about St Peter Mancroft sounded rather like a schoolboy's ode to a totem pole: it was, *'old, big and has a lot of carving on it.'* In this he was at odds with Nikolaus Pevsner, with whom he had co-edited the 1960s volumes on Sussex and Surrey for *The Buildings of England*. Pevsner – who thought Nairn's contributions too subjective – judged St Peter Mancroft, *'the Norfolk parish church par excellence'*; John Betjeman thought it was superb; and in his *'England's 1000 Best Churches'* Simon Jenkins wrote, *'Few who enter St Peter's for the first time can stifle a gasp.'*

The only other building in Norwich *'with the authority of the cathedral'* was St James Yarn Mill on the Wensum, built in 1843 to give a boost to our waning textile trade. Nairn's first wife worked for local printers and booksellers Jarrolds, whose printing works were then in St James Mill and according to architectural historian Gillian Darley it was Nairn's intervention that gained the building its Grade I listing in 1954.

As he was penning words of praise about this temple of industry Nairn was using his other hand to take a swipe at, *'the intricate antics of the city's interminable late-Gothic churches.'* Norwich has so many medieval churches, more than any other city north of Rome – something to glory in yet anathema to Nairn. He was selective and sparing with his approval. He did like the interior of St George Colegate but only because its Gothic fittings had been replaced with unfussy Georgian.

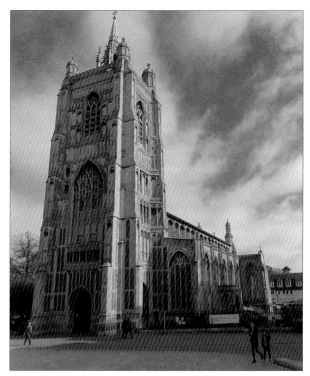

St Peter Mancroft

Within spitting distance of St Peter Mancroft (far too close for a dyspeptic critic) is Norwich City Hall, completed in 1939 in a style influenced by Stockholm's City Hall and Concert Hall. You might have expected Nairn to admire Norwich City Hall's freedom from fuss. Instead, he found it timorous and lacking commitment. Once again he was out of step with Pevsner who considered the project to be an architectural triumph that would go down in history as one of the foremost English public buildings of between the wars.

Nairn summed up City Hall's personality defects by comparing, *'the empty bombast of the lions in front ... with their C12 prototype in Brunswick.'* Both are stylised, both are things of beauty but in calling the Norwich lions bombastic Nairn struggles to find focus for his general antipathy. What exactly did Norwich do to him? The poor old Norwich lion does have a slicker hair-do than its German relative but it was installed at a time when the City Council was demolishing hundreds of medieval slums and looking forward to the streamlined kind of future promised by modern Swedish architecture.

Norwich City Hall

The Norwich Lion 1938

The Brunswick Lion 1170. Public Domain

Magdalen Street bisected by the flyover

Nairn revisited Norwich in 1967. He wrote: *'The highlight of 1965 was the approval of a proposal by the City Engineer to build a flyover exactly half-way down that recently famous Magdalen Street; meanwhile, a property company has bought up large chunks of 'old rubbish' to the north; the character of Coslany has finally gone.'* Scroll forward to find that lovely old Magdalen Street was not improved by the structure that was meant to save it, for the flyover destroyed Stump Cross (the heart of Norwich-over-the-Water) and effectively broke the street in two.

As for Nairn's chunks of old rubbish behind Magdalen Street, the St Augustine's area was bulldozed in order that Norwich could be given its own emblem of urban revitalisation – the pedestrian precinct. The problem was that pedestrians had a long walk from the city centre to a satellite from which they were notionally excluded by the new inner ring road. Unloved, Anglia Square became a collection of downmarket discount stores, the multi-storey carpark closed, the excessive surface parking around the uncompleted development was simply tatty, and Sovereign House – the project's Brutalist flagship – was abandoned by Her Majesty's Stationery Office.

Around the time of his second visit to Norwich, Nairn was falling out of love with new architecture, using the front of the Observer's Review to shout: *'Stop the architects now. The outstanding and appalling fact about modern architecture is that it is not good enough.'* The lesson learned from 70 years of post-war town planning is that open urban space needs to be on a human scale and in tune with the historic environment if it is to be loved. It is therefore hard to comprehend why plans have been submitted to redevelop Anglia Square with a 25-storey tower. Whether it is 25 or a concessionary 20 storeys high is immaterial since any tall tower, plus three large 12-storey blocks, will be cruelly out of scale with the surrounding Conservation Areas. If this development goes ahead, and Nairn were to return to his great town view from St James' Hill, he would see the Cathedral spire no longer unchallenged but going head-to-head with an uninspiring monolith. (Approved 2018 by the City Council: denied 2020 by the Secretary of State).

Sovereign House, Anglia Square

Nairn's Norwich essay in 'Nairn's Towns' introduced by Owen Hatherley (Notting Hill Editions, 2013). I also recommend, 'Ian Nairn: Words in Place' edited by Gillian Darley and David Mackenzie (Five Leaves Publications, 2013).

One of Norwich's well-rehearsed claims is that it was first (1608) to establish a library in a building owned by a corporation and not by church or school. As these caveats suggest, most libraries up to this point were monastic. Like other cathedrals, Norwich Cathedral had a library but it does not pass down to us intact for it was destroyed twice: first by citizens in the Tombland Riot of 1272, then again during Henry VIII's Dissolution of the Monasteries (1538).

Before the advent of printing (c.1450), the volumes would have been manuscripts, hand-written on parchment. From the original cataloguing marks, it has been estimated that 120 of about 1350 pre-Dissolution books remain in the Cathedral Library. Other Norwich books ended up in Oxford and Cambridge including the spectacularly illustrated Psalter given to the Priory in the 1330s by the Norwich monk, Robert of Ormsby. Another Norfolk treasure of the fourteenth century is the Gorleston Psalter, once in Norwich Cathedral Priory now in the British Library.

After the Dissolution, the city assembly agreed in 1608 that three rooms in the 'New Hall', which were rented to its sword-bearer, Jerrom Goodwyne, should be converted into 'a lybrary for the use of preachers, and for a lodging chamber for such preachers as come to this

The Gorleston Psalter c1301-326 Public Domain

Blackfriar's Church, by Wenceslas Hollar C17. The library was housed in the building lower left. Public Domain

cittie'. By 'New Hall' the city fathers meant Blackfriars' Church, purchased for the city by Augustine Steward, and known today as The Halls. This new library stood at the south porch of St Andrew's Hall.

The donors' book gives the founder of the library as Sir John Pettus (c1549-1614), the Mayor in 1608. Although he bequeathed a small collection of books to the library, Pettus left no funds for its further development. This seems to have set the pattern for the piecemeal acquisition of books down the years for there is little evidence that the Assembly paid for anything other than the occasional volume.

After the Reformation, the foundation of a City Library could be viewed as part of the transfer of knowledge and power from Church to local government, but this was no secular enlightenment for the library was set up to provide lodging for itinerant Puritan preachers. At the invitation of the city administration, preachers delivered 'the word' at the green yard in the Cathedral precinct, their sermonising assisted by the wide range of sectarian tracts they would have found at their lodging place.

After some years of neglect the Old City Library was re-founded in 1657, by which time its scope had broadened to include secular topics such as philosophy, law, mathematics, maps, county guides etc. Donations were evidently eclectic: the library did not possess Newton's monumental Principia – which included his laws of motion and ground-breaking ideas about gravity – but it did have Galileo's System of the World in which he supported Copernicus' observation that the earth was not the centre of the universe but rotated around the sun, not vice versa. For expounding this heretical idea

Galileo had been placed under house arrest by the Inquisition in his home near Florence. The presence of Galileo's System in the Norwich City Library signifies a more liberal climate in Protestant England.

The extraordinary degree of self-government granted to the City of Norwich over the years by the Crown generated a sense of independence and radicalism. Political nonconformity was accompanied by a rise in dissent against the established church and by the early eighteenth century around 20% of the city's population were Protestant dissenters. Prominent among these was the surgeon, Philip Meadows Martineau whose name is commemorated by Martineau Lane near County Hall. He and his niece Harriet Martineau worshipped in the Octagon Chapel in Colegate.

The Octagon Chapel, Colegate

In 1784, Philip Martineau proposed the founding of a subscription library. This may have been in reaction to the increasing Anglicanism of the City Library over the preceding century, for the new committee of 24 contained only five clergymen. As a sign of more enlightened times, 26% of the original subscribers were women. Subscribers also had the keys to the Old City Library and the two libraries soon merged. Despite being supported by private subscription the

Galileo, by Justus Sustermans, 1636 Public Domain

Haymarket Picture House, 1959 ©georgeplunkett.co.uk The site of the N&N Literary Institution

Some years before this move there had been criticism of the running of Norwich Public Library: complaints such as the absence of standard works, lack of new titles, failure to raise the annual subscription, and a librarian with a disobliging manner. In 1822 a break-away faction suggested setting up their own library. The Norfolk and Norwich Literary Institution – of which William Unthank was a shareholder – opened at Haymarket Hill on New Year's Day 1823. These two subscription libraries were to run in parallel for over half a century.

In 1838, the Literary Institution's deserted partner, the Norwich Public Library, moved to new premises on the site of the old city gaol on Guildhall Hill. When I wrote the blog post the building was occupied by The Library, a restaurant that subsequently closed.

new institution was rather confusingly named the Norwich Public Library and, indeed, claims by the various offshoots to represent 'Norwich' or the 'Public' make the head spin. In 1794 this growing library moved 150 metres to the disused Catholic chapel of the Duke of Norfolk's Palace on St Andrew's Street where it remained until the library moved again in the 1830s.

The Norwich Public Library, St Andrew's Street, 1936 ©georgeplunkett.co.uk

Guildhall Hill Subscription Library, 1955 ©georgeplunkett.co.uk

For a time, the original Public Library had custody of books from the old City Library but they were poorly kept and the council threatened to move them to their rival, the breakaway Literary Institution. The problem was eventually solved when a third library – this time a truly public, free, non-subscription library – was built in 1857. The 1850 Libraries Act allowed larger boroughs to add up to half a penny in the pound to the rates to pay for library facilities and staff. Norwich Council was first to adopt the Act, Winchester was first to form a library under the Act but Norwich was first to construct its own Free Library. This opened in 1857 at the corner of St Andrew's (Broad) Street and Duke Street. The Act did not allow for the purchase of books so the volumes inherited from the old City Library, which had started out in St Andrew's Hall, were to provide an important nucleus for the embryonic library.

The photograph by George Plunkett shows the Public Library in 1955, the council having dropped the word 'Free' in 1911. To the right, but just out of sight, was the Duke of Norfolk's Chapel that once housed the 'Martineau' Norwich Public Library after it moved from St Andrew's Hall.

For a while the top floor of the Free/Public Library had been an unsatisfactory home for the Norwich School of Art until it moved to the Technical Institute on St George's Street. Towards the end of its life, the library was used as a shoe factory and in 1963 it was demolished to give way to the new Central Library in Bethel Street. Demolition allowed the widening of St Andrew's Street, the better to aid the flow of traffic out of the city, over the Duke Street Bridge and down to the inner link road. The corner site is currently occupied by a British Telecom telephone exchange, set back from the original building line.

Former site of the library at St Andrew's and Duke Street

St Andrew's Street Free Library, 1955. ©georgeplunkett.co.uk

And what of the two subscription libraries? The libraries that had uncoupled in 1822 decided to come together again; in 1886 the Norfolk and Norwich Literary Institution joined the 'Martineau' Norwich Public Library in their premises on Guildhall Hill to form the Norfolk and Norwich Library. But just twelve years after

Central Library, Bethel Street 1962. © georgeplunkett.co.uk

The Forum houses the N&N Millennium Library

this merger, a fire that started in a nearby rope-maker's on Dove Street spread to the warehouse of Chamberlin and Sons' department store on Guildhall Hill and gutted the adjacent library. Most of the library's 60,000 volumes were destroyed, including collections held by law, naturalist and archaeological societies. The restored library was reopened in 1914 and closed in 1976, when many of its books were given to Norwich School.

Fire also plays a part in the continuing story of the City Library. The Free/ Public Library built by the council at the corner of Duke/Exchange Street in the mid-nineteenth century was demolished in 1963 when the new Central Library – designed by City Architect David Percival – was opened on a site between City Hall and the Theatre Royal. In August 1994 this library was destroyed by fire, much as the subscription library on Guildhall Hill had been destroyed nearly a hundred years before. Over 150,000 books were burned along with irreplaceable historical documents from the Record Office.

In 2001 The Forum, designed by Michael Hopkins and Partners, arose from the site of the fire-damaged library, facing St Peter Mancroft. The Norfolk and Norwich Millennium Library, which is housed in The Forum, has been cited as the busiest library in the UK.

Norwich has fine suburban libraries, such as the twentieth century branch libraries at Earlham and Mile Cross, but its first branch library was in one of the city's oldest buildings. This was the Lazar House in Sprowston, a Norman chapel and leper hospital founded by the first Bishop of Norwich, Herbert de Losinga (d 1119). After local antiquarian Walter Rye rescued the building from destruction in the early twentieth century it was presented to the city by Sir Eustace Gurney and served as a branch library from 1923 to 2003.

The Lazar House, Sprowston

Two architects changed the face of Victorian Norwich: Edward Boardman sketched out the quiet fabric of a post-medieval city, its offices, factories and churches, but it was George Skipper who provided the fireworks.

George Skipper age 69. Photo: Richard Barnes

The son of a Dereham builder, Skipper (1856-1948), spent a year at Norwich School of Art studying art and – probably at his father's insistence – architecture. He followed the architectural path but, as the Norwich Mercury wrote in 1906, he was known for his 'artistic temperament' and he expressed this side of his personality in the exuberance of his buildings. He is reputed to have said, you *"need an artist for a first rate building."* However, when Skipper and his brother won the commission to build Cromer's town hall (1890) it was with a sober version of the fashionable Queen Anne Revival style that gave little indication of the pyrotechnics to come. This modest building announced Skipper's habit of buying-in decoration, in this case the terracotta carvings by James Minns from the Gunton Brothers' Brickyard at Costessey.

Cromer Town Hall

Cromer was to prove a useful source of work for George Skipper. In the late 1880s Clement Scott's column *'Poppyland'* in the Daily Telegraph extolled the virtues of the North Norfolk coast, particularly around Overstrand. The book based on these articles, *The Poppyland Papers*, was hugely popular and this, combined with the arrival of the Great Eastern Railway in 1887, transformed nearby Cromer from a quiet fishing village to a fashionable watering place for the wealthy. As a young boy Winston Churchill had visited the town and reported back to his mother, *'I am not enjoying myself very much'*.

The comfortable middle and upper middle classes, who came to see the coastal attractions, needed somewhere appropriate to stay. This triggered a wave of hotel building and a consortium of Norwich businessmen engaged Skipper to design several. After The Grand Hotel he built The Metropole, which is said to have shown signs of Skipper's flair and exuberance but both hotels were demolished, as was another of his hotels, The Imperial. The last vestiges of the Hotel Metropole Hotel are the letters HM on a back gate off the High Street.

Hotel de Paris, Cromer

designed what is now the Marks and Spencer building in Norwich. Skipper transformed the Cliftonville into an example of the eclectic Arts and Crafts style with glimpses of Queen Anne Revival and French Renaissance. Externally, there are terracotta art nouveau panels and ogee pepperpots while, internally, the stained glass panels in the dining room doors depict poppies to remind Clement Scott's readers of where they were. Skipper's first offices (1880) in Norwich were in Opie Street but by 1891 he was employing about 50 people and in 1896 he moved to larger premises at 7 London Street (now part of Jarrold Department Store). At a time when architects were not allowed to advertise their services, Skipper sailed close to the regulatory wind by commissioning Guntons to sculpt terracotta plaques depicting his trade. In the background of the carved panel that we saw in the chapter on 'Fancy Bricks' are three of Skipper's large Norwich projects: The Daily Standard Building in St Giles' Street (1899); Surrey House for Norwich Union (1904); and Commercial Chambers (1901) in Red Lion Street.

Fortunately for us, one of Skipper's best known projects survives. This is the Hotel de Paris (1896) for which Skipper disguised the existing Regency facade with a frontage reminiscent of the late medieval palace at Chambord. The roofline is punctuated with turrets and pepperpot cupolas that he used throughout his career, even using this device to disguise an ugly lift heading at Sandringham. The architectural commentator Marc Girouard thought the Hotel de Paris was cruder but jollier than Skipper's other hotels.

Further along the clifftop at Cromer is another survivor: The Cliftonville Hotel. It was originally built to the designs of Norwich architect, AF Scott, who

Commercial Chambers, Red Lion St.

Poppyland glass, Cliftonville Hotel

As an architect, Skipper drew on a variety of sources. The French Renaissance style of his early years was enriched by Flemish influences from his visit to Belgium as a student but for his prestigious projects he provided a more weighty Neo-Classical Palladian style. This can be seen in the Norfolk and Norwich Savings Bank (now Barclays Bank) in Red Lion Street, the Norwich and London Accident Assurance Association (now St Giles House Hotel in St Giles' Street) and his most expensive and sumptuous project, Surrey House for Norwich Union Life Insurance Society (now Aviva). Pevsner and Wilson thought Surrey House was, *"One of the country's most convinced Edwardian office buildings."* The central Marble Hall built by two teams of Italian stonemasons is spectacular, decorated with marble originally destined for Westminster Cathedral.

But Skipper still found time for more playful ventures in which he flirted with British Art Nouveau. The Royal Arcade is one such transitional adventure, as we shall see in the following chapter.

Hints of Art Nouveau were to be seen amongst the turrets and domes of the Norfolk Daily Standard offices (1899-1900) on St Giles Street. This highly decorated building, faced in faience (glazed ceramic ware), survived the bombing of the adjacent building in 1942 but later lost some of its features during a conversion to a Wimpy Bar. In response to 'exuberant' buildings such as these the Poet Laureate and founder member of the Victorian Society, John Betjeman, wrote his well-known quote in the foreword to the Norwich School of Art's catalogue for their 1975 exhibition on Skipper. Betjeman said, *'He is altogether remarkable and original. He is to Norwich rather what Gaudi was to Barcelona.'* But let's not forget he was big in Cromer, too.

The Marble Hall, Surrey House

Norfolk Daily Standard offices, St Giles' St.

A more convincing example of Skipper's Art Nouveau tendency is the Royal Norfolk and Suffolk Yacht Club at Lowestoft. Skipper's competition-winning design from 1902 is stripped of the decoration and frenetic eclecticism of his other projects to produce a building using, *'the vocabulary of British Art Nouveau ... with more than a sidelong look at CFA Voysey'* – this from David Jolley and Edward Skipper in their 1980 appreciation of George Skipper. Voysey's influence can be seen in the sloped buttresses relieved by circular and semi-circular windows and plain stucco walls topped off by a copper dome. Free of extraneous decoration, this puritanical excursion was a one-off for Skipper.

To make way for the new tramways, the east side of Red Lion Street was demolished in 1899. As a result, its replacement provides snapshots of turn-of-the-century design, all built in a single campaign by Skipper and Boardman. Skipper's Commercial Chambers in Red Lion Street (1901-3) is wedged into a narrow site between his Norfolk and Norwich Savings Bank (1900-3) and Edward Boardman's veterinary premises designed for John Pollock (1901-2). This narrow frontage, clad in faience (probably by Doulton), is decorated with statues of children. This busy decoration is continued up to the skyline where Skipper creates interest by using moulded cornice, statuary, a finial and a campanile that just sneaks above Boardman's adjacent Dutch gable by the height of its copper dome.

Lowestoft Yacht Club. Photo: David Bussey

Roofline of Skipper's Commercial Chambers

George Skipper at Commercial Chambers

Because Commercial Chambers was built for the accountant Charles Larking you might think that the robed figure making entries into a ledger at the top of the building was Larking himself but it is clearly the self-publicist Skipper with his generous moustache.

In stages, from 1896 to 1925, Skipper remodelled the frontage of Jarrold's department store at the corner of London and Exchange Streets. Original plans show that Skipper had also planned a trademark dome to surmount the semi-circular bay at the front corner of the building but, by the end of this long project, no copper-clad dome materialised. Work began first on the London Street side whose second floor facade is punctuated by a series of Royal Doulton plaques bearing the names of authors first published by Jarrold Printing. Perhaps the only name familiar to modern readers is that of Anna Sewell, who wrote *Black Beauty* while she lived in Old Catton, to the north of the city.

Skipper's plans for a dome were again frustrated, this time for the London and Provincial Bank (1907) a little further along London Street. Architectural interest was created by breaking the flat symmetry of the classical facade with a fourth bay. This bay contains a semi-

'The tiered wedding cake' of the city's favourite store

London & Provincial Bank in 2016

Skipper houses in College Road

circular, two-storey bay window that breaks through the deep cornice capping the facade. This device makes sense when we learn that Skipper had originally planned to top the fourth bay with one of his cupolas whose circular section would have matched the curved segment of the cornice. Unfortunately, the cupola was abandoned because it would have infringed a neighbouring property's right of light.

Just before the First World War, Skipper had planned to retire but the loss of his savings invested in the East Kent Coal Board meant he had to keep working. After the war his work in Norwich seems largely confined to humble plans for roads and sewerage required to open up the area of the Golden Triangle around Heigham Park and College Road (where he also designed neo-

Georgian buildings). Further afield, he designed various buildings in Norfolk, Kent and London and in 1926 built a second extension to the University Arms Hotel in Cambridge. Here – perhaps harking back to his heyday – he did successfully add two cupolas although the result was felt to be incongruous.

During the Second World War Skipper had kept his London Street offices open while his son Edward, a fellow architect, was on active service. Edward could not, though, afford to keep the offices open and in 1946 he sold the building to Jarrolds. As Edward Skipper and Associates, the firm went on to design public housing in the city. George Skipper died in 1948 when he was 92 and is buried with his first wife in Earlham Cemetery.

Towards the end of the nineteenth century, artists across Europe were breaking away from the academic tradition to form a new art known variously known as 'le style moderne', Jugendstil (youth style), Secessionism, Stile Liberty, Style Mucha, all gathered under the general banner of Art Nouveau. A surprising example is found in Norwich.

Most variants of Art Nouveau exaggerated the organic curves of plants that had echoes of the reversed curve or the ogee seen in medieval church architecture. But even at this early stage, the sinuous line of the fourteenth century English Curvilinear period appears less full-blooded than the continental version in which the line reflexes back on itself to produce the flame-like curves of the Flamboyant period.

Curvilinear west window, St Mary Snettisham, Norfolk
Creative Commons CC BY-SA 2.0

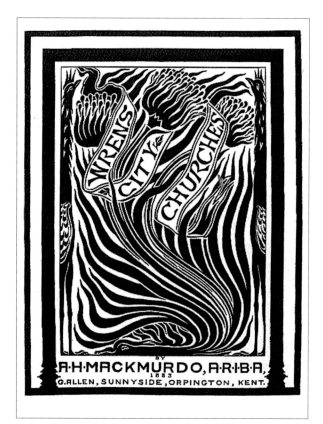

Cover, Wren's City Churches. AH Mackmurdo Public Domain

According to Nikolaus Pevsner, the first time that the flexuous line can be identified as an example of late nineteenth century Art Nouveau was in a book cover by the English designer Arthur Heygate Mackmurdo (1851-1942) published in 1883 . At about that time Mackmurdo incorporated a similar swirling design into the splat of an otherwise conventional chair. Unlike the sinuous tracery in church windows of the Curvilinear period, which were either radially or bilaterally symmetrical, Mackmurdo's design was asymmetrical. He was evidently pleased with the outcome and we can see its influence in a design for a fabric named 'Cromer Bird': Hurrah for Norfolk.

The 'Wren' book cover might imply that Art Nouveau originated in Britain but in reality the new art was an amalgam of styles that emerged at about the same time across Europe and America. Despite Mackmurdo's pioneering spirit it would be a mistake to imply that Britain led the way in Art Nouveau design for this country was timid – certainly in terms of building – in expressing the pent up energy of the whiplash line to be seen in French and Belgian versions of the new style. Perhaps it was felt to be too sensuous, too Continental, too Catholic? Only in Scotland do we see a more widespread adoption of florid Art Nouveau by the Glasgow School, especially in the fabric designs of the Glasgow Girls.

Mackmurdo chair 1883-4
Photo: paulreeveslondon.com

A rare example of the Continental style of Art Nouveau in England is The Royal Arcade in Norwich, designed by architect George Skipper. Unlike the decorative 'Castle' entrance from the Back-of-the-Inns, the classical frontage at the Marketplace end, which remains from the previous Royal Hotel of 1864, gives no clue to the exotic interior. The awkward layout of the stables and yard of the old hotel created a problem for Skipper for he didn't have a straight run from front to back. He tried to disguise the slight dog-leg by placing a roof lantern at the middle, which marked a break in the southern run of bow-fronted shop fronts where a short side alley connected with White Lion Street. At the Castle end of the arcade, Skipper incorporated a preexisting Bullards pub, which became the Arcade Stores. Doulton tiles helped blend this side-shoot with the main arcade but the ornate window didn't survive the conversion to a butcher's shop in 1963

The Royal Arcade

Royal Arcade 1935 ©georgeplunkett.co.uk

Edward Everard building, Bristol. Public Domain

William Caxton.Norfolk Daily Standard building

Daniel Defoe. Norfolk Daily Standard building

Skipper laid out the bare bones of the structure but it was WJ Neatby's colourful tiles that provided the Art Nouveau influence, leading Rosemary Salt to say that the arcade was like a *'fragment from the Arabian Nights dropped into the heart of the old city.'* His façade to Edward Everard's printing works in Bristol, built about the same time, 1900, is similarly clad in colourful pictorial (Doulton) tiles and is another fine example of British Art Nouveau.

The figure to the left on the Everard building is the inventor of the printing press, Johannes Gutenberg: to the right is William Morris who revived the art of printing with his Kelmscott Press. This resonates with the Norfolk Daily Standard offices in St Giles' Street, illustrated in the previous chapter. Another Skipper gem, that building is decorated with Doulton brown terracotta tiles. Although there are minor Art Nouveau touches it is not really an example of the movement for its influences are more eclectic. But recalling those two figures on the Everard building, and the tendency of architects to borrow a good idea, the Norfolk Daily Standard building bears portraits of William Caxton (the first English printer) and Daniel Defoe (usually credited as the author of the first English novel).

Neatby had been head of Sir Henry Doulton's architectural department for about ten years when he designed these projects. Doulton had made his money from the glazed stoneware pipes that helped improve

A reminder of The Angel Hotel

Parian Ware peacock

London's sanitation. He also supported a more artistic use of the medium by employing students from the nearby Lambeth School of Art to produce Doulton Art Pottery. Neatby was responsible for decoration applied to buildings and experimented with a form of pottery that would mimic Italian marble. This result was Carraraware, with a dense white body, which was used to clad the exterior of the Royal Arcade. Look up above the east entrance and see the white winged angel made of Carraraware, a reminder of the Angel Hotel that preceded the Royal (a new Royal Hotel was built by Boardman on Agricultural Hall Plain).

For the interior, Neatby employed Parian Ware, a kind of biscuit porcelain better known for making busts and statues but here it was glazed in brightly coloured Art Nouveau designs. The peacocks that run in a frieze above the windows, the inverted heart-shapes and the sign for the Conservative Club are all made from large tiles with raised outlines to contain the bright glazes. To make these Neatby had to pour enamel glazes into indentations impressed into the mould as it was formed – a technique that was said to be exceedingly difficult.

The best examples of Art Nouveau are in the spandrels of the arches supporting the central light well. Here, the figures – composed of flat tiles – show a poster-style image of a woman holding a circle that, in original sketches reproduced in the Proceedings of the Society of Designers (1900), contained a sign of the zodiac.

Tiles in central light well

Salome, poster. Alphonse Much 1897
Public Domain

A junkshop find

A possible influence for this image of the young woman comes from Alphonse Mucha's 1897 poster of Salome holding what seems to be a circular harp. Many years ago I bought a framed tile from a junk shop in Cambridge; the buff-coloured base is a large-format sanitary tile stamped 'Doulton' on the back. It has no other imprints to indicate this was painted at the Doulton factory and could be a blank painted by an amateur, perhaps at an evening class. When writing the original blog post I realised that the woman from the tile was copied, in reverse, from Mucha's Salome.

Whatever the influences, Skipper never produced such a colourful building again and we shouldn't forget WJ Neatby's contribution to this local masterpiece.

Cartoon for Norwich Arcade, WJ Neatby Proc Soc Designers 1900

It was WJ Neatby's application of tiles that transformed George Skipper's Royal Arcade into a rare example of Art Nouveau architecture in this country. In *The Buildings of England*, Pevsner and Wilson hit the nail on the head when they described it as *'a spectacular display of English Arts and Crafts, when, in spirit though not in form, it came nearest to Continental Art Nouveau ...'* They said that *'only two commercial buildings deserve a place in any book on* (the Arts and Crafts) *in England: the Royal Arcade ... and Fastolff House in Regent Street, Great Yarmouth...'* This took me to Yarmouth in search of the unpublicised tour de force.

Front elevation

Fastolff House

Architect, Ralph Scott Cockrill, named Fastolff House (1908) after SIr John Fastolff – Shakespeare's Falstaff – who was born not far away in Caister Castle. This Merrie England reference is appropriate for a building with bands of casement windows designed with Norman Shaw's Old English Revival in mind. The underlying structure of this building is therefore more decidedly Arts and Crafts than the Royal Arcade and Edward Everard's printing works in Bristol although all three become Art Nouveau through the application of tiles. But where the Norwich and Bristol buildings achieve their stunning appearance by the use of

Neatby's polychrome tiles, Fastolff House is clad in a facade of monochrome grey faience whose effect depends upon deep under-carving instead of two-dimensional illustration.

RS Cockrill's father John William, who was Borough Engineer for Great Yarmouth 1890-1903, held a joint patent with Doulton's of Lambeth for a process in which glazed ceramic tiles were used as shuttering into which concrete could be poured. This was not the method used on Fastolff House but the association with Doulton suggests that they could have supplied the carved faience tiles. Unfortunately, it is not possible to prove an association between Fastolff House and Doulton since the tile-maker's archive has suffered over the years from fire and flood.

The carved foliage on the Yarmouth building has been likened to Germanic Art Nouveau. It is true that German and Austrian Art Nouveau, like the British, resisted the excesses of the sinuous 'whiplash' line that characterised the Belgian and French versions. 'The British style' can be seen in the bird and tree patterns of CFA Voysey, in Archibald Knox's Art Nouveau

NOV.
15 '98

VOL. 15
No. 68

Front cover of The Studio magazine

designs for Liberty tempered with his Celtic Influences, and in Charles Rennie Mackintosh's more restrained and geometric version. However, for a prototype we need look no further than the cover of the progressive decorative arts magazine, The Studio.

Great Yarmouth's second Art Nouveau building by RS Cockrill is The Hippodrome (1903), one of only two purpose-built, permanent circus buildings remaining in Britain. Here, the decorative surface is provided by buff-

A Voyseyesque panel

coloured terracotta moulded with various Art Nouveau motifs. If only the birds would look at each other the decorative panel would be a fair copy of Voysey's birds-in-a-tree design – a popular favourite disseminated widely on textiles and wallpaper.

RS Cockrill's Hippodrome

In the second part of my riverside walk I made a passing mention to My Lord's Gardens, a reminder of the presence of the Dukes of Norfolk in the city. As we saw, the Howard family fell in and out of favour according to the religious leanings of each passing monarch. When Charles II restored their dukedom, Henry Howard re-established the family's connection with Norwich by commissioning the gardener and diarist, John Evelyn, to design him a pleasure garden between King Street and river. This was to be the first pleasure garden outside London and the first of several such public gardens in Norwich. In 1776, some 100 years later, the gardens were still marked on Samuel King's map as was the adjacent Spring Gardens.

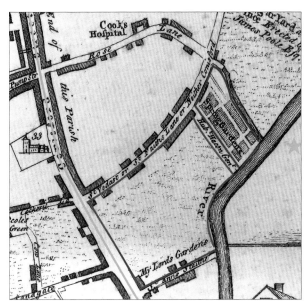

My Lord's Gardens outlined in red, Spring Gardens in blue.
Green line = King's Street. Star = present-day rail station.
Samuel King's map of 1766 courtesy Norfolk County Council.

The Sixth Duke started to rebuild his family's palace near the present-day Duke Street Car Park but there was a lack of recreational space here. To compensate for this, Evelyn's garden was laid out on the other side of the city. Around 1663 the duke paid £600 for a plot on the site once occupied by the Austin Friars off King Street. Throughout the 1700s Norwich was one of a handful of cities, like Bath and Tunbridge Wells, where the rising 'middling rank' could enjoy provincial imitations of London's fashionable pleasure gardens.

Descriptions of My Lord's Garden are scant. Dr Edward Browne (son of Norwich philosopher Sir Thomas Browne) said they contained: *"a place for walking and recreations, having made already walkes round and crosse it, forty foot in breadth. If the quadrangle left bee spatious enough hee intends the first of them for a fishpond, the second for a bowling green, the third for a wildernesse, and the forth for Garden."*

In 1681 Thomas Baskerville arrived at the garden by boat and ascended *"some handsome stairs"* to be served *"good liquors and fruits"* by the gardener. He saw a fair garden with a good bowling-green and many fine walks. Although we have no image of the garden in those early days it is possible to get an impression from Samuel and Nathaniel Buck's 1741 *'Prospect of Norwich from the South-East'*. Looking towards King Street from the Thorpe side, this prospect shows the area in the bend of the river occupied by formal gardens. The dominant feature is the formal parterre of what appear to be hedges and/or small trees arranged in linear walks,

Samuel and Nathaniel Buck's south-east prospect of Norwich 1741
Courtesy Norfolk County Council

some diagonal, separated from the houses on King Street by densely-planted trees. However, the map's key reveals the barely visible '9' at the centre of the parterre to be Spring Gardens rather than My Lord's Gardens. This isn't consistent with Samuel King's map that shows My Lord's Gardens to occupy most land and to extend some distance eastwards around the river bend. Either way, the engraving illustrates the essential formality of gardens at that time.

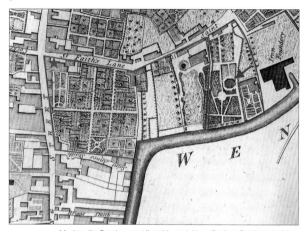

My Lord's Gardens outlined in red, New Spring Gardens in blue
Howard House is starred; arrow indicates the Pantheon
Hochstetter's plan (1789) courtesy of Norfolk Record Office

The Bucks' prospect, possibly romanticised, is also out of kilter with Anthony Hochstetter's plan of 1789 indicating that My Lord's Gardens extended well around the river bend. Hochstetter shows the portion of My Lord's Gardens nearest King Street to be comprised of a cluster of rectangular plots, some crossed by delineated walkways. The large untreed space could be the bowling green, known to be still around in 1770, and might the rest have been redesigned for its new role as a public garden now that the Duke of Norfolk had abandoned the city for Sussex?

As in King's map, Hochstetter's also illustrates Spring Gardens adjoining My Lord's Garden. In 1739, gardener John Moore had designed New Spring Gardens as a place of quiet pleasures where ladies and gentlemen could enjoy wines and cider, cakes and ale; they could also promenade or take a pleasure boat ride on the river. Those formal walkways were still visible on Hochstetter's map. Of My Lord's Gardens, the only reminder is the recently renovated Howard House and the extant flint wall on King Street, which photographer of mid-twentieth century Norwich, George Plunkett, suggested could be the original boundary wall of the Austin Friars.

Howard House and possibly original boundary wall, 1934. ©georgeplunkett.co.uk

Moore had named his garden after London's New Spring Gardens, which were mentioned by Samuel Pepys and later – when renamed Vauxhall – visited by Becky Sharpe in Vanity Fair. Following fashion, Norwich Spring Gardens were renamed Vauxhall Gardens. Initially, Moore's was a rural garden where people could stroll through, *"a very curious Transparent Arch built in the Gothick taste"*, no doubt aping London's Vauxhall. But in 1768, in response to competitors, Moore's widow began illuminating the garden and entertaining guests with music and fireworks. Around 1776 the gardens were acquired by James Bunn, performer and scene painter from the Theatre Royal, which gives an idea of the increasing theatricality now expected of public pleasure gardens. What had started as a fashionable stroll had become commodified entertainment. Now, public gardens featured performance.

Over the winter of 1776/7, Bunn started to build a 1000-seater Pantheon, named after the building on London's Oxford Street (demolished in 1937 and now the site of Marks and Spencer). The original Roman Pantheon, and its London relative, is circular but the Norwich version appears on Hochstetter's plan as an octagon; this was to offer new all-weather attractions.

Throughout the latter quarter of the eighteenth century there was increasing competition between Mr Curtis of the old My Lord's Gardens and Widow Smith of Spring/ Ranelagh Gardens. Fireworks featured heavily: Curtis introduced line rockets and public breakfasts but the widow raised the stakes by employing a Mr Quantrell as engineer. He was to take over the garden.

Smaller gardens were scattered around the city but the third major pleasure garden was situated on Butter Hill between Bracondale and King Street, high above present-day Carrow Bridge. This was The Wilderness, leased to Samuel Bruister in 1748. His wrestling matches initially attracted an ungenteel clientele but The Wilderness raised its sights and in a few years was able to compete with New Spring Gardens. During Assize Week, when circuit judges came to town and the city

The Walk inside the city wall, down to the Black Tower

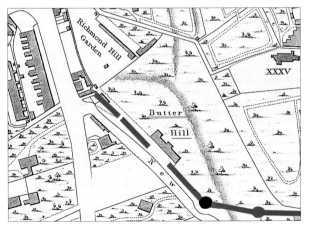
Butter Hill or The Wilderness Gardens
City walls at the top of Carrow Hill in red, Bracondale in yellow
Millard & Manning's map 1830 courtesy of Norfolk County Council
Norfolk Heritage Centre Collections

was open for entertainment, they began by providing public breakfasts and music. However, when part of The Wilderness was re-opened as Richmond Hill Garden ca 1812 it was primarily as a venue for fireworks.

In practical terms a 'wilderness' suited the hilly terrain above King Street but it was also more in tune with ideas of naturalistic landscape expounded by Capability Brown. Just inside the city wall on top of Carrow Hill it is still possible to see the gravelled Long Walk, along which visitors would stroll down to the Black Tower (later a snuff mill).

The fourth, and probably most popular, pleasure garden was situated between present-day Sainsbury's supermarket on Queen's Road and the St Stephens roundabout. Widow Smith's Rural Gardens started

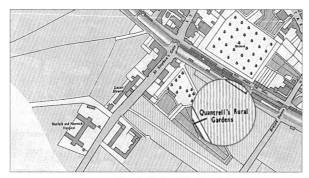

Quantrell's Rural Gardens. ©The Historic Towns Trust

will turn round its Axis, and fall into four parts, and will discover Vulcan inside, who will be attended by his Cyclops ... Vulcan's (pyrotechnic) Cave and Forge and the Eruption of Mount Aetna." When Spring Gardens poached Signor Pedralio, Quantrell's riposte was to employ his own Italian pyrotechnician, Signor Antonio Batalus, who would, *"Fly across the Garden with Fire from different Parts of the Body."* Who wouldn't pay good money to see that?

After the first flight of a manned balloon was made in France in 1783, England experienced Balloon Mania. The following year Mr Bunn's balloon floated quite happily inside his Norwich Pantheon, but he made the mistake of leading it outside where it was quickly lost in a shower of hail. In 1785, Quantrell won this contest by hosting an actual balloon ascent by Norwich man James Decker with a 13-year-old girl as passenger. The balloon was damaged in a squall, Miss Weller was left behind but Decker ascended and came down safely near Loddon. In his diary, Parson Woodforde mentions that the balloon passed over him as he stood on 'Brecondale' Hill.

And it was from Quantrell's that Major John Money made his famous balloon flight in 1785. In trying to raise

around 1763 as a nursery garden but when the widow began to illuminate the grounds on Guild Days and to sell cider and nog, she set two men at the gate to keep out disagreeable persons. She also employed William Quantrell as engineer for her firework shows and before long he owned Quantrell's Gardens. Competition between the various gardens was intense: My Lord's Garden had installed complex machinery to represent land and sea battles; The Wilderness had a *"grand Piece of Machinery ... to run 680 Yards upon a Line"*; but Quantrell had Signor Pedralio's *"Globe 21 feet in Circumference which*

Major Money's Perilous Situation. Public domain via Wikimedia Commons

122

funds for the nearby Norfolk and Norwich Hospital on St Stephen's Road, the major took off only to be carried away by an 'improper current'. He descended into the sea off Yarmouth in which he was immersed for seven hours before rescue.

At the end of the eighteenth century, Quantrell's Gardens came into the hands of Samuel Neech who renamed it Ranelagh Gardens after the pleasure gardens in Chelsea. From Canaletto's grand painting of the London resort it is hard to believe that its Norwich counterpart was anything like as ambitious. But Neech was soon to add to its attractions by buying The Pantheon from the defunct Norwich Spring/Vauxhall Gardens and erecting it on his own site, next to his Amphitheatre.

Pablo Fanque House in All Saints Green

The dying notes of the Ranelagh Gardens' existence will bring joy to anyone familiar with The Beatles' music. Just before it closed, the Gardens had contained a circus operated by William Darby of Ber Street, known as Pablo Fanque. Fanque was the first black circus owner and is mentioned in *'Being for the Benefit of Mr Kite'* from the Sergeant Pepper album. His name is also commemorated in the new Pablo Fanque House, which provides student accommodation on All Saints Green.

In addition to the Big Four, other smaller pleasure gardens grew up around Norwich in the nineteenth century. Some were tea gardens, others were attached to public houses. These included: The Mussel Tea Gardens in Telegraph Lane, Thorpe; The Greyhound Gardens

on the east side of Ber Street; The West End Retreat, Heigham; The Gibraltar Gardens, Heigham Street – all providing breathing space from the crowded city with its insanitary 'yards'. In 1815, balloons were still in fashion at Prussia Gardens, Harford Bridge – now the Marsh Harrier. A Mr Steward took off but only *'skimmed and skimmed and skimmed and skimmed'* (a single word can be so expressive), to stop 500 yards away. In World War One some soldiers removed the pub sign bearing the King of Prussia's head, prompting the patriotic change of name to the King George.

Pleasure gardens provided leisure and entertainment to the public for well over a century. The specific demise of Norwich's Ranelagh/Victoria Gardens offers a clue to the disappearance of pleasure gardens in general. In 1849, Ranelagh Gardens (known as Royal Victoria Gardens since 1842) were closed and sold to the Eastern Union Railway Company whose Victoria Station was to be one of three in Norwich. The railway company built platforms either side of The Pantheon as we shall see in the chapter that follows. This pleasure garden was therefore subsumed beneath the railway that changed the public perception of affordable leisure by offering city-dwellers access to healthy seaside resorts.

The Marsh Harrier at Harford Bridge

One of the pleasures of posting a blog article is that readers sometimes reply to fill in the gaps. This certainly happened with the post on Norwich pleasure gardens. The Pantheon had just been an ambiguous shape on a 200-year-old map but railway enthusiast Bill Smith was to provide details that brought it back to life.

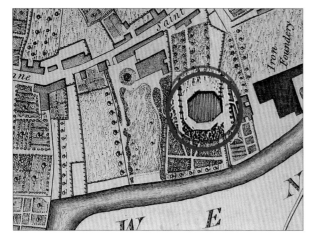

The Norwich Pantheon (enlarged). at New Spring Gardens
Hochstetter's map 1789
Courtesy of Norfolk County Council, Norfolk Heritage Centre Collections

First, a brief recap of what we know about the Norwich Pantheon that we glimpsed in the preceding chapter. The 1000-seat Norwich Pantheon was erected in New Spring Gardens (later called Vauxhall Gardens) on the riverside behind King Street. In appearance we only know from Anthony Hochstetter's map of 1789 that the Norwich Pantheon was originally octagonal. Cole's map of 1807 confirms the shape. However, Cole seems to have blindly copied this part of Hochstetter's map since the Pantheon had been absent from the riverside for a number of years.

In the 1790s Samuel Neech bought the defunct Vauxhall Gardens and used the building materials from The Pantheon to construct a new rotunda in his Ranelagh Gardens, just off the present-day St Stephens

Dome of the Pantheon, Rome

roundabout. Now, the resurrected Pantheon could accommodate 2,000 persons, twice its original capacity, allowing the gardens to offer fashionable entertainment throughout the year and in all weathers. The name was undoubtedly retained, not so much to acknowledge the prodigious Roman Pantheon with its 141-feet-diameter domed roof , but for James Wyatt's London Pantheon (1772 - 1937). This place of public entertainment was said to have been the most elegant building in Europe. Could Norwich's version have rivalled this?

Masquerade at the Oxford St Pantheon, London. Public domain via Wikimedia

Victoria Station 1913. Image: Norfolk County Council Library and Information Service

In 1849 the Ranelagh (later, the Victoria) Gardens were bought by the Eastern Union Railway Company who repurposed the existing buildings for their Norwich terminus, which was one of three railway stations in the city. Fortunately, Norwich Victoria Station survived well into the twentieth century so there are photographs of what may be the old Pantheon, now used as a booking office. Instead of a dome it had a conical roof with glass panels at the apex and, as we might have guessed, it was a homeopathically-diluted version of its London archetype.

Two weeks after I published the post on pleasure gardens, a railway enthusiast – Bill Smith – queried whether this photograph could really show the fabled Norwich Pantheon. It reveals the domed roof of the booking office to be roughly circular in section, in contrast to the distinct octagon that Hochstetter had drawn for the original site. Might it therefore be a different building, such as the 'amphitheatre' that a previous owner is said to have constructed eight years before the Pantheon appeared on the site?

Ranelagh Gardens off present-day St Stephen's roundabout. Hochstetter's map 1789. Courtesy of Norfolk County Council, Norfolk Heritage Centre Collections

Hochstetter's plan of 1789 shows no large buildings on the Ranelagh/Victoria site while the 1830 map by Millard and Manning indicates that before the coming of the railway there was only one large building in Ranelagh Gardens. The sketchy drawing is ambiguous. It could either be described as an octagon with a small extension at front and a larger extension at the back or could that central portion be square with rounded corners? Those rounded corners turned out to be useful in reimagining the Norwich Pantheon.

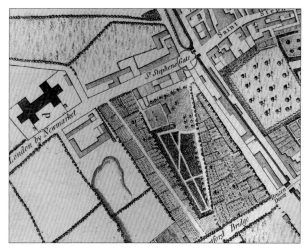

Ranelagh Gardens 1830. Millard & Manning's map
Courtesy of Norfolk County Council, Norfolk Heritage Centre Collections

In 1905, by which time Ranelagh/Victoria Gardens had become Victoria Station, Bill Smith identified the main garden building wedged into the V between two diverging platforms.

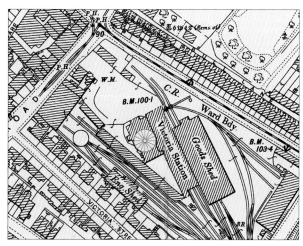

Ranelagh Gardens building in Victoria Station courtesy of Bill Smith
© Ordnance Survey map 1905

On the detailed 1880 OS map, Bill was able to scale the rotunda to fit two circular segments of the building (remember those 'rounded corners') and, using the 56½-inch gauge of the railway tracks as a standard, he calculated the rotunda's diameter at around 74 feet. This was approximately half the diameter of The Pantheon in Rome.

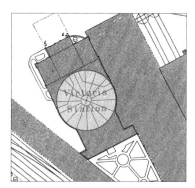

Rotunda roof scaled to building by Bill
Smith. © Ordnance Survey map 1880

The photograph from inside the booking office also showed that the conical roof with its central light was 16-sided – just enough sides to approximate a circle at its base. And Bill demonstrated that the roof sat on what was almost certainly a circular rotunda, not an octagonal one or even a hexadecagonal one. Samuel Neech may have recycled material from the old Norwich Pantheon but he didn't stick to the original's eight-sided floor plan.

Bill's reconstruction strongly suggests that The Pantheon was the large circular building so if there was an 'amphitheatre' it had to be something else. Supporting this, local historian Trevor Fawcett had written that when the railway company took over the gardens in 1849 the platforms were laid either side of the Pantheon while the Amphitheatre (a rectangular building at front) became the ticket office and luggage room. This arrangement can be clearly seen in an old postcard, with the conical tip of the Pantheon's just visible behind the Amphitheatre at front.

The Victoria Station lingered on until the 1960s, creating the opportunity for aerial photography to confirm the arrangement of a circular Pantheon separated from the St Stephen's Road entrance by the Amphitheatre at front. But one year after the end of World War Two

an aerial shot lets us see into the station complex, now roofless, probably as a result of enemy action. This provided a fortuitous glimpse into the largest surviving building from the era of Norwich's pleasure gardens. Another reader, Grant Young, found an even better view of the station from above, which Bill Smith outlined to show the main compartments, see opposite.

With this plan in mind we can now walk ourselves through the rooms of the Ranelagh/Victoria Gardens as described by The Norfolk Chronicle of November 1849:

"Two sides of the spacious area which presented itself on passing the entrance, to the west and the north were occupied with "boxes", or "arbours", where parties could sit, and enjoy their refreshments, or sip their wines, while they listened to the instrumental or vocal music ... On the South, was a large room ... used as a "Nine-pin-room". It opened into a spacious and excellent bowling green. To the eastward, and nearly in the centre, of the grounds, stood a building, called 'The Pantheon'. Over the entrance was an orchestra; and on each side of the entrance-passage were rooms, from the windows of which refreshments were supplied. The passage led to a spacious and lofty saloon, often converted into a ballroom; beyond this was an arena, which was, in the Assize-weeks, used as a Concert-room; at other times it was occasionally used as a circus ... and anon a theatre ... Beyond the Pantheon, the grounds were tastefully laid out, and several walks for promenading were constructed ... The palmy days of these gardens is now fading fast ... but there was a time, when they were the resort of our fashionable aristocracy; and the public breakfasts ... were amongst the most gay and pleasant assemblages, that it was ever our good fortune to encounter."

TWO Bs, OR NOT TWO Bs?

NORFOLK'S THOMAS JECKYLL

Norfolk's Thomas Jeckyll was a largely unsung hero of the nineteenth century Aesthetic Movement whose popularization had its roots in Norwich. I first came across his work when I bought the catalogue to an exhibition that brought together the various branches of this diffuse group. The peacock and sunflowers on the front cover were dominant themes in Jeckyll's output.

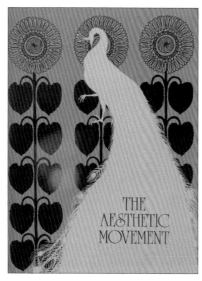

The Aesthetic Movement (1973). Ed, Charles Spencer. Academy Editions London

Thomas Jeckyll and father 1860s
Image: Norfolk County Council Library and Information Service

Thomas was the son of George Jeckell, curate at the abbey church of Wymondham. He was fascinated by church architecture, restored many churches in the county and, under the wing of his sponsor Sir Thomas Boileau, designed new additions to Ketteringham Church, Ketteringham Hall and the surrounding estate. He also designed a canopy over a memorial statue for Lady Boileau (d. 1862), sited at the junction between the Newmarket and Ipswich Roads. The structure was later demolished but Sir Joseph Boehm's statue – said to have been based on a younger Lady Boileau – was re-sited some 100 metres away where it can still be seen in the grounds of the former Norfolk and Norwich Hospital.

For a while Jeckyll had an office on Norwich's Unthank Road but, like his friend the painter Frederick Sandys, whose work is represented in the art gallery at Norwich Museum, he fancified his name with a 'y' and moved to London. There, Jeckyll joined a group of aesthetes spearheaded by Arch Dandy, James Abbot McNeill Whistler. These artists were enthralled by the artefacts coming out of a Japan forced out of seclusion by American gunboat diplomacy of the 1850s.

The avant garde competed for Japanese porcelain and prints: Whistler is even said to have fought over a

Boileau Memorial Fountain. Newmarket/Ipswich Road

Japanese fan. The virtual absence of linear perspective from Japanese prints inspired the 'flattened' poster art of Toulouse Lautrec, Alphonse Mucha and Aubrey Beardsley while Gustav Klimt clothed his models in bright patterns influenced by his collection of Japanese kimonos. This was high art but industrialisation allowed Japanese imagery to be imported into ordinary homes on an unprecedented scale. A search around antique centres will still turn up Victorian transfer-printed crockery decorated with roundels, cherry blossom, fans and cranes. In this sense, the Anglo-Japanese Aesthetic Movement contrasts with the anti-mechanisation, pro-handmade ethic of William Morris' Arts and Crafts Movement.

Japanese motifs on English china

When I first bought a house in Norwich, many years ago, the previous owner told me that the front gate had been made from ironwork salvaged from an old structure in Chapelfield Gardens, which I presumed to be the pagoda built by Barnard Bishop and Barnards . In 1876, Barnards had exhibited a cast-iron pavilion at Philadelphia; in 1880, the Norwich Corporation bought the pagoda for £500 and erected it in Chapelfield Gardens, surrounded by a fence comprised of 72 iron sunflowers, three feet six inches tall. Even though sunflowers had no special connection with Japanese art they became emblematic of the Aesthetic Movement in general, as seen on the front cover of the exhibition book.

In 1942, Norwich was badly bombed in the Baedeker Raids, so-called because targets of cultural and historic importance were chosen from Baedeker's tourist guide for the effect they would have on civilian morale. The pagoda is said to have suffered blast damage that, together with general corrosion, led to it being

Chapelfield Pagoda, the sunflower railings enlarged. Courtesy of Sarah Cocke

dismantled in 1949. This was a matter of great regret for the city lost something magical. Some of the sunflowers were saved to be reused on a fence at the tennis courts in Heigham Park then refurbished in 2004 for the park gates. Copies of the iconic sunflower were made with one layer of petals, rather than the original two layers, and these can be seen at the gates to Chapelfield Gardens.

My garden gate contained no sunflowers but it did hold two roundels, each embossed with two butterflies, head to head, antennae locked. This was how designer Thomas Jeckyll marked his work for Barnard and Bishop's Norfolk Ironworks and it's reasonable to suppose that the butterflies' initials 'b' represented the initials of the firm's owners, Barnard and Bishop. Nothing is left to remind us of their ironworks in Norwich-over-the-Water except a modern housing development named Barnards Yard. Jeckyll also designed for them the Norwich Gates that won praise in international exhibitions and were then bought by public subscription to be given as a wedding present to the Prince (later, King Edward VII) and Princess of Wales. The imposing gates are now at Sandringham. These masterworks were not 'Aesthetic' but other gates that Jeckyll designed for Sprowston Hall are clearly in the Japanese style. The seigaiha pattern, otherwise

known as the Japanese 'blue ocean wave' design, provides the basis for the Sprowston gates, studded with his roundels, some decorated with his 'two-butterflies' symbol.

Jeckyll's gates for Sprowston Hall, butterfly motif enlarged

Jeckyll's butterflies have been confused with moths but, unlike butterflies, moths don't have bulbs at the end of their antennae nor do they have on their wings the 'eyes' of the peacock's tail that give name to the peacock butterfly. It is this two-butterfly logo that characterises Jeckyll's work for Barnard and Bishop. In 1859, Charles Barnard's two sons joined the firm, which became known as Barnard, Bishop and Barnards (note 'Barnards' plural), and Jeckyll's Aesthetic fireplaces started to appear embossed with four insects (bees) and/

The two-butterflies motif on a cast-iron fireplace

Four bees symbol

Four insects, four Bs and 'N' for Norwich

or four capital letters (Bs). One variation shows four indeterminate insects forming a square, surrounding four capital Bs with the letter N (for Norwich) at the centre. Evidently, Jeckyll enjoyed picture puzzles.

When he renovated Ketteringham St Peter's church in the 1870s Jeckyll personalised it with an Aesthetic Movement sunflower and two stone butterflies carved into a boss on the tower. The stone is rather weather-worn but it is still possible to make out the interlocking antennae. This tells us that in his architectural practice, which was independent of his work for Barnards, Jeckyll retained the 'two butterfly' mark as his own.

Two-butterflies boss on tower of Ketteringham church

A high point of the Anglo-Japanese Aesthetic Movement is Whistler's 'Harmony in Blue and Gold: the Peacock Room', now in the Freer Art Gallery, Washington. It started life as a room in Kensington designed by Jeckyll for the wealthy collector, Frederick Richards Leyland, to display his blue and white Chinese porcelain. The room was lined with embossed leather said to have been imported by Catherine of Aragon but now accepted to be eighteenth century Dutch leather from Old Catton Hall, on the northern outskirts of Norwich. But Jeckyll was going through an acute phase of manic depression, a familial condition from which his father suffered. Jeckyll spent some time in Heigham Hall, a private home for mental illness, then moved to the Bethel Hospital in Bethel Street, where he died in 1881.

In Jeckyll's enforced absence, Whistler – whose own signature was a rather overwrought butterfly – took charge of the project. He had been working on other rooms of Frederick Leyland's mansion and had been consulted on colour schemes in Jeckyll's room. But with Jeckyll in Norwich, Whistler went far beyond any agreement with Leyland: he overpainted Jeckyll's leather surfaces with blue and green and gold, even gilding his shelves. Admittedly, he did this rather brilliantly and because of the gold-embossed peacocks it is generally referred to as Whistler's Peacock Room. Jeckyll's contribution was eclipsed and his friend Sandys is said to have exchanged words with Whistler about this. The only signs of Jeckyll's involvement are the two gilded andirons in the fireplace, in the form of the Aesthetic sunflowers we now see in Heigham Park and Chapelfield Gardens.

The Peacock Room at the Freer Art Gallery. Public domain

When I visited Norwich School in early 2020 I was shown a medallion of Amelia Opie in her high Quaker bonnet. The frame, as much as the medallion, tells us a surprising amount about Amelia's life and the Norwich in which she lived.

Mrs Opie's medallion. Courtesy Norwich School

I call her Amelia because that's what her biographer, Ann Farrant , called her. Despite this precedent I walk on eggshells since she was a stickler for the correct form of address: '... *do not call me Mrs Amelia Opie. I am not Mrs Amelia Opie but Mrs Opie or among friends Amelia Opie ... Mrs Opie, Norwich is my lawful and proper designation.*'

On the medallion, beneath the sitter's shoulder, is inscribed the single name 'David' – like a rock star. Napoleon was known by just the one name and the only contemporary artist with sufficient celebrity to be known by a single name was Jacques-Louis David, the foremost painter in revolutionary France. The medallion's David, however, refers to the sculptor Pierre-Jean David, from the town of Angers, who made medallions of more than 500 well-known figures. When Pierre-Jean entered

the studio of Jacques-Louis David he differentiated himself from his patron by adopting the name of David D'Angers.

After Britain and France declared peace in 1802 Amelia travelled to France. As the granddaughter of a dissenting minister, daughter of a doctor with radical sympathies, and travelling with companions who supported the French Revolution, there seems little doubt that Amelia had come to see France's new society for herself. In the group was her husband, John Opie RA (1761-1807), one of whose attractions as a suitor was that he'd agreed to live in the Opie household if Amelia proved averse to leaving her beloved father and the house on Colegate where she was born. She was to outlive him by 46 years.

John Opie self-portrait 1794, aged 33. Dulwich Picture Gallery

Pierre-Jean David D'Angers, aged 67. Bibliothèque Nationale de France

Amelia had been taught French by her great friend, the Reverend John Bruckner from Leiden in The Netherlands, who was pastor to the city's French-speaking Protestants at St Mary-the-Less in Queen Street (and, later, to the Dutch Strangers in Blackfriars' Hall). She is said to have insisted that John Opie paint a portrait of Bruckner as a condition of their marriage.

Amelia was obsessively interested in Napoleon and managed to see him twice at close quarters. But two years later Amelia became an unbeliever when Napoleon snatched the crown from the Pope, placed it on his own head and declared himself Emperor. As she said, *'The bubble burst.'*

It had been thought that Amelia met David D'Angers on this visit but her biographer, Ann Farrant, makes it clear that it wasn't until 1829, when Mrs Opie was a widow

and a Quaker with a high Quaker bonnet, that she first met D'Angers and formed a strong friendship with him. She was pleased that he had captured her likeness on the medallion, noting that he'd contrived to make the Quaker bonnet look a little like the classical Phrygian cap worn by the French revolutionaries as their bonnets rouges.

Freeman's label on back of medallion

On the back of the medallion is a label, 'From Freeman's. Repository of Arts 2 London Street. Norwich.' The business was founded by Jeremiah

Freeman but the Freeman at the time of the Opie medallion would have been his son William (1783-1877). He is listed as proprietor of a 'General Furnishing Warehouse and Repository of Arts' at Number Two London Street. But to describe Freeman as a warehouse proprietor would be to seriously underestimate his business for he employed 63 men, women and apprentices producing furniture and gilt frames of the highest quality. He made gilt and gesso furniture in the rococo style for Norfolk's grand country houses, including Felbrigg Hall and Blickling Hall. As a frame-maker he would have been in competition with Norwich School artist James Thirtle who is known to have made frames for his brother-in-law, John Sell Cotman. Three generations of Freemans were embedded in the artistic life of the city. Jeremiah (1763-1823) was President of the Norwich Society of Artists in 1818 – a

Back of the Opie medallion with enlarged 'Noverre'?

post held by William himself two years later. William's son, William Philip Barnes Freeman (1813-1897), went to Norwich School with John Crome's son and was taught drawing by John Sell Cotman. And in 1854 the first meeting of the Norwich Photographic Society was held on their premises.

In addition to Freeman's label on the reverse of the medallion, a faded copperplate inscription has been preserved: *'Amelia Opie cast from a macet (i.e., maquette or model) by David of Paris during her visit in April (and here the original paper is torn). Presented by Wm Freeman Magistrate to the N …'* but this and the following tangle of pale letters are difficult to decipher. The final line has just the date,'1851', two years before Amelia's death. My first impression was that the difficult-to-decipher word beginning with 'N' was 'Noverre'. This turned out to be incorrect but, as my old maths master insisted, I'll show my workings, since the digression opens a small window onto contemporary Norwich society.

The Noverres were a Swiss-French Protestant family who lived in The Chantry adjacent to the Assembly House. Augustin had been ballet master at Drury Lane Theatre London, with David Garrick while brother Jean-George, back in France, had been dancing master to Marie-Antionette. One evening, just as he left the stage, Augustin

Overmantel mirror by Wm Freeman ca 1825. Courtesy Paul Farrelly

was caught up in an anti-French fight. He mistakenly thought he had run an assailant through with a sword and fled to Norwich where he is said to have been sheltered by French Huguenot silk weavers.

Augustin's British-born son Francis (1773-1840) came to Norwich to teach dance, deportment and aspects of cultural refinement required by those aspiring to join Georgian polite society. He built the west wing of the Assembly House for his ballroom. Long before she became a Quaker, the adolescent Amelia was an enthusiastic dancer; a friend recalls dancing 'from seven to eleven' at a reception for Prince William Frederick held at Amelia's father's house. John Opie painted a portrait of the two Noverre children so it's almost certain that Amelia knew of the Noverres.

Public assemblies in the Assembly Rooms were not, however, all stately minuets and cotillions for at the end of the evening the ladies would retire to remove the hoops from their skirts in readiness for country dancing. Some thought country dances tedious: standing still for half an hour as long lines of paired dancers took their turn to run

The Assembly House

the gauntlet. But, as historian Marc Girouard described, in order to do this 'the double doors between ballroom, card-room and tea-room were opened up, and country dances danced along the lengths of all three rooms'. You would have to have a heart of stone not to enjoy cavorting with your partner down the whole 143 feet beneath candle-lit chandeliers.

'A Country Dance' by Wm Hogarth. Wellcome Images

Restored inscription, 'Norwich' underlined

At some stage, the original inscription on the reverse of the Opie medallion was glued to a new backing without closing the horizontal tear that runs along the penultimate line. On a print, I cut out the tear and joined the original edges. What I'd unconfidently construed as 'Noverre' could now be seen to be part of 'Norwich'; however, the short final word (4-5 letters, florid italic capital, perhaps an abbreviation) defeated my crossword-solving app and left Mr Freeman's intention opaque.

As a young woman Amelia became a well-known author, publishing several novels and works of poetry. She was intellectually curious and made friends with Lady Caroline Lamb, Mary Wollstonecraft (*A Vindication of the Rights of Women*), Sir Joshua Reynolds, JMW Turner, Richard Brinsley Sheridan, Maria Edgeworth and sister Norvicensian Elizabeth Fry. In 1825, as a woman in her mid-fifties with both husband and father

Bust of Amelia Opie 1836, by David D'Angers. Norwich Castle Museum and Art Gallery

Amelia Opie 1798, by John Opie RA. National Portrait Gallery, London.

There is a description by Miss Thackeray, daughter of William Makepeace Thackeray, of a lost photograph of Amelia, '… *in her Quaker dress, in old age, dim, and changed, and sunken, from which it is very difficult to realise all the brightness, and life, and animation which must have belonged to the earlier part of her life...*'. Some of this youthful spark was captured by John Opie in 1798, just after he and Amelia were married.

This was the painting on which Mrs Dawson Turner, wife of Yarmouth banker Dawson Turner, based her slightly prettified etching of Amelia in 1822. Long before she renounced fashion and adopted plain Quaker garb the 21-year-old Amelia had published an anonymous work on the Dangers of Coquetry. It therefore comes as a surprise to learn that she requested the Norwich School painter Joseph Clover to ask Mrs Turner to modify the likeness. Mary Turner went through five iterations before Amelia was satisfied. Although I don't show this etching I do show Lucy Knights' mural of Amelia Opie in Norwich Market (2019), which seems to be based on the Turner engraving. One hundred and sixty six years after her death it is this image of a vibrant, unbonneted woman that endures.

dead, Amelia joined the Society of Friends. Now she was free to worship in the Friends' Meeting House in Upper Goat Lane instead of her father's chapel, the Octagon in Colegate.

Amelia's staunch support for the abolitionist cause is likely to have originated with her mother who, after her parents had died, became very attached to her black nurse. Amelia's name headed a list of 187,000 women petitioning for the end of slavery and in 1840 she was one of the few women to be represented in Vintner's engraving, held in the National Gallery, of those attending the 1840 Anti-Slavery Society Convention. She cuts a distinctive figure in her high Quaker bonnet – the bonnet depicted in the Norwich School medallion. The profile reappears on the marble bust by David D'Angers forming the centrepiece of a display of anti-slavery artefacts in Norwich Castle Museum and Art Gallery.

Amelia Opie from a mural on a Norwich Market stall, by Lucie Knights

In Spring 1999 I took part in an alternative sculpture-trail, visiting unexpected art in public spaces: pieces hidden in plain sight, works that had outlived their original purpose, and unseen eroticism in a monument to a national heroine. 'Open Secrets: Unexpected Art in Norwich', was led by Krzysztof Fijalkowski, a young lecturer – now professor – from the Norwich School of Art. Here, I retrace some of our steps and add a few of my own.

'Open Secrets' walk

First stop was at the Cavell statue outside the Erpingham Gate to the Cathedral. Born in nearby Swardeston, Edith Cavell was a nurse during WW1. In 1915 she was shot by a German firing squad in Belgium for assisting the escape of Allied prisoners and – according to former head of MI5, Dame Stella Rimington – for espionage. Notes in the printed tour guide (price 20p) gave a post-Freudian interpretation of the Cavell Memorial, mentioning the placement of the soldier's erect rifle and the wreaths that mark Cavell's breasts.

A few days later, the Eastern Daily Press cartoonist, Tony Hall, published a cartoon in which the soldier takes one of the stone wreaths to strike the young lecturer on the head for his scandalous interpretation.

"Sorry Dr Fijalkowski.– didn't quite catch that last bit, about why you think this monument is scandalously erotic . . . ."

Eastern Daily Press May 20 1999 ©Tony Hall

The Cavell Statue. Originally outside The Maid's Head (L)
Beside the Erpingham Gate (R)

Not far away we visited a curved mural, tucked away from passers-by at the east end of London Street. Boldly commissioned in 1974 by the Norwich and Abbey National Building Society, Tadeusz Zielinski's 'Symbol of Norwich' depicts a modern family, sheltered under the Society's roof, against the background of the walled city with its cathedral. The modernist treatment is reminiscent of the Festival of Britain style of the early

Zielenski's 'Symbol of Norwich'

Thorn's murals. Courtesy of Emily Duke

1950s but any obscurity of meaning will only have been increased by Betfred's logo that – drilled and screwed into the artwork – now blocks the first row of panels. Aaaagh!

Who, when buying half a pound of six inch nails in Thorns the ironmongers in Exchange Street, has failed to notice the wall paintings on the first floor? When I visited the ironmongers, many years after the sculpture trail, an assistant moved some ladders for me to see some of the murals protected behind Perspex screens. Emily Duke, a member of the Paston family who were partners of the founder RE Thorn, told me that before the hardware business was opened in the early nineteenth century the building had been a hotel in which an artist painted the rooms in return for accommodation. The figures are clothed in a variety of costumes and seem to represent People of All Nations.

The redundant St Laurence's is amongst five churches along St Benedict's Street. It has one of the most prominent towers in the city yet it, and the west doorway, are easy to miss as you concentrate on the precipitous steps down St Laurence's Passage. Stop half way down to see the spandrels above the west door depicting two gruesome deaths: the roasting of the eponymous saint on a gridiron and East Anglia's St Edmund riddled with Viking arrows. His head was thrown into a forest but rescuers were guided to it by a Latin-speaking wolf crying hic, hic, hic. The head of the wolf can be seen, bottom right.

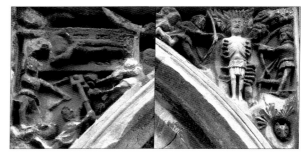

Laurence and St Edmund at St Laurence's Church

High above Orford Hill stands a statue of a stag placed there towards the end of the Victorian period but what we see now is a fibreglass replica from 1984. Exactly what it was advertising was much easier to guess when a bold wooden sign, 'GUNMAKER', advertised the trade of occupants George Jeffries followed by Darlows. Since we walked the sculpture trail the stag's antlers have shed a few branches and the Gunmaker sign has disappeared. I can remember the Gunmaker sign but younger generations won't and things that seemed fixtures become orphaned by time.

Peter Hide's 'Girder Structure'

Darlow & Co, gunmaker, 1938. ©georgeplunkett.co.uk

Another stop on the trail was to see one of the first purchases by the Norfolk Contemporary Art Society in 1978. At the time, this work by a former lecturer at the School of Art, Peter Hide, was situated on a piece

of wasteland behind the Duke Street carpark. Hide seems to have intended this as a formal exercise in 'horizontality' and balance but, once out of the studio, works of art take on meanings of their own. In its original site, looking across the river to a Victorian ironworks, the girders provided an incidental link with our industrial past. Since our guided walk, the piece has been transplanted to a spot just off the busy St Crispin's roundabout where it gains a new layer of interpretation – one of the perils of (re)siting sculpture in a public setting. The Girder Structure is now near the former site of one of the city's three railway stations: City Station. Here, it can be seen as a memorial to the terminus of the Midland and Great Northern railway that was bombed in the 1942 Baedeker raids and closed in 1959.

Next, some examples from my own travels around the city. At the corner of St Stephens and Surrey Streets, opposite Marks and Spencer, is a postwar block decorated with identical stone carvings hidden beneath the keystones of the three curved window arches. Even if you can discern them without the aid of a zoom lens (and I couldn't) it isn't immediately obvious what these

Postwar commercial block, St Stephen's Street, with boar's head inset

Boar's Head Inn, after 1900

animals might signify. What they commemorate is the previous occupant of this site – the ancient Boar's Head public house, destroyed by a Baedeker raid in April 1942. The present postwar building, like the rest of the south side of St Stephen's Street, was set back to widen the street. The alley behind this building, named Boar's Head Yard, is a further reminder of the late medieval pub. In a flea market I found an old postcard of this thatched inn, bearing the surname of the nineteenth century licensee, Richard Norgate of Cawston.

The same air raids destroyed a basket-maker's shop on nearby Ber Street. The reconstructed building is currently occupied by Gerald Giles' home electricals store but the wooden carving on the tympanum above the door is a residue of an earlier post-war life. The panel by Joseph Lloyd Royal depicts dockers unloading ships, suggesting that the building may once have been a warehouse for storing goods from Norwich docks. Until the 1980s the Wensum was still navigable by quite

large vessels that would reverse direction at the wider turning basin, a little south of the railway station. The Norfolk and Norwich Agricultural Hall (now occupied by Anglia TV), at the top of Prince of Wales Road, is built from alien Cumberland sandstone. The heavy keystones above the ground floor windows are carved in red brick, probably by James Minns and his son who were 'carvers' at Guntons Brick Yard in Costessey. Some carvings appear to depict generic mythical figures while others seem to be specific portraits but I can find no record of their identities. The triple feathers clearly refer to the Prince of Wales, who supported the rebuilding the Norwich and Norfolk Hospital. The Prince of Wales feathers also signify the road itself, which was

Ships Unloaded' by JL Royal, opposite John Lewis

built to connect Norwich Thorpe station with the agricultural markets around the castle. The bull's head offers another decipherable allusion. Once you recognise the name of local philanthropist JJ Colman on the foundation stone it is impossible not to see the beast as a reference to the trade mark on tins of Colman's mustard.

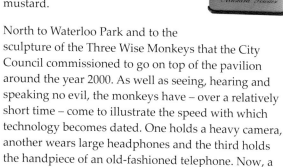

North to Waterloo Park and to the sculpture of the Three Wise Monkeys that the City Council commissioned to go on top of the pavilion around the year 2000. As well as seeing, hearing and speaking no evil, the monkeys have – over a relatively short time – come to illustrate the speed with which technology becomes dated. One holds a heavy camera, another wears large headphones and the third holds the handpiece of an old-fashioned telephone. Now, a monkey with a smartphone could do all three jobs.

Traces of past use can be seen all around the city. I am especially fond of mosaics that decorated the thresholds of shops that were household names in my childhood. Magdalen Street has two good examples.

The initials, FH&W, were used as a symbol to advertise national shoe chain Freeman Hardy and Willis in the 1960s. It had been the biggest shoe manufacturer in the country but by the 1990s the chain had disappeared, broken up by the British Shoe Corporation. In the face of foreign competition Norwich's once ascendant shoe trade was going the same way.

Another mosaic advertised the Maypole dairy chain who were known, paradoxically, for promoting non-dairy margarine. As well as marge, which was popular amongst the working class, they focused on eggs, tea, condensed milk and butter. Around 1930 they had more than 1000 stores but due to narrow margins and fierce competition they began to lose business and the last store was closed in 1970.

Maypole in Magdalen Street

1. Late eleventh century Norwich Cathedral has the largest monastic cloister in England.

2. The Cathedral has over one thousand roof bosses, more than any other religious building in the world.

3. 'Revelations of Divine Love' by the anchoress Julian of Norwich (c1342-c1416) is believed to be the first English book written by a woman.

4. The city's defences, comprised of the river and fourteenth century city walls, enclosed an area larger than the City of London.

5. Norwich has more churches than any other city north of the Alps.

6. Norwich's Guildhall (1413) is the largest medieval civic building outside London.

7. St Andrew's Hall is the most complete surviving friar's church.

8. William Cuningham's 1558 map of Norwich is the earliest surviving map of any town or city outside London.

9. Church Alley, immediately south of St Augustine's church, contains the longest row of Tudor cottages in England.

10. The Sixth Duke of Norfolk's pleasure garden (My Lord's Garden) was the first outside London (1660).

11. In 1608, Norwich was first to establish a library in a building owned by a corporation and not by church or school.

12. The Norwich Post (1701-1713) is believed to be the earliest truly provincial English newspaper.

13. The Norwich Society of Artists, established in 1805, was the first provincial art group.

14. In 1819 the Rosary became the first cemetery in the country where anyone could be buried irrespective of religion, without having to be supervised by an Anglican minister.

15. Harriet Martineau (1802-76) is considered to be the first female sociologist. She was one of the first female journalists and probably first to make a living from writing.

16. Norwich-born Pablo Fanque (1810-1871) was the country's first black circus proprietor.

17. Norwich was the first to adopt the 1850 libraries act and to construct its own free library.

18. At Colman's factory in 1878, Phillipa Flowerday became the first industrial nurse in the country.

19. Around 1900, Howlett and White's shoe factory in Colegate was the largest in the country.

20. Nikolaus Pevsner, in his Buildings of England, considers Norwich City Hall to be 'the foremost English public building of between the wars'.

21. Norwich City Council was the first local authority to install a computer to deal with the rates system (1958).

22. In 1959, Magdalen Street was the first of the Civic Trust's redecoration schemes to revive postwar streets.

23. The first trials of Royal Mail postcodes took place in Norwich in 1959.

24. From 1985-9, Ana Maria Pacheco was Head of Fine Art at Norwich School of Art and was the first woman to hold such a post in the UK.

25. The Norfolk and Norwich Millennium Library is the most visited in the UK.

26. In 2010 The John Innes Centre and the Sainsbury Laboratory at Colney topped a worldwide survey of the most influential scientific papers published in plant and animal sciences.

27. In 2012 Norwich was rated the most godless city in the country.

ACKNOWLEDGEMENTS

First, I owe an enormous debt of gratitude to my friend
Karen Roseberry for designing this book and transforming
the scrolling format of the website into pages.

It is difficult to imagine a web-based book, especially a
history book, without numerous images. I have benefitted
greatly from George Plunkett's archive of photographs
of a vanishing Norwich, managed by his son Jonathan
(www.georgeplunkett.co.uk). I am also indebted to the
Norfolk County Council's 'Picture Norfolk' website and
Clare Everitt (https://www.norfolk.gov.uk/libraries-local-
history-and-archives/photo-collections/picture-norfolk).
Thank you, too: Broadland Memories, Richard Barnes, The
Burrell Collection Glasgow, David Bussey, Ann Christie,
Sarah Cocke, Paul Cooper, Roger Cullingham, Rosemary
Dixon of the Archant Archives, Emily Duke, Paul Farrelly,
Brian Gage, Tony Hall, Paul Harley, Simon Knott, Peter
Mann, Mike Page, Paul Reeves, Sue Roe, Sanders of Oxford,
Bill Smith, Alan Theobald, Grant Young. All have provided
ideas, photographs, permissions or, in the case of my wife
Sue, a gimlet eye.

We are fortunate in Norfolk to have excellent resources
for historical research. In researching this book I was
enthusiastically assisted by the staff of The Norfolk Record
Office, The Norfolk Heritage Centre at the Norfolk and
Norwich Millennium Library, and the Norwich Castle
Museum and Art Gallery.

To all, thank you.